Remembering Freedom

Connor Curley

New Harbor Press
RAPID CITY, SD

Curley/New Harbor Press
1601 Mt. Rushmore Rd, Ste 3288
Rapid City, SD 57701
NewHarborPress.com

Ordering Information:
Quantity sales. Special discounts are available on quantity purchases by corporations, associations, and others. For details, contact the "Special Sales Department" at the address above.

Remembering Freedom/Connor Curley. —1st ed.
ISBN 978-1-63357-483-0

Contents

A Note on the Text

English is a very hard language to philosophize in. Our modern political climate makes it even more so. To avoid potential misinterpretation, it is necessary to include here a note on the intrinsically gendered grammatical structure of the English language.

English's default is to the masculine. Pronouns intended to describe a group of people, or a person in general (gender non-specific) are referred to with male descriptors. This is basic grammar, and while modern linguists may be attempting to change this feature of English, the language at this time is still masculine by default. You will note that I follow this grammatical rule in the text: when referring to humans *as* humans, I say Man, or he. To alleviate misinterpretation, however, when referring to Man as in a member of the species *human*, I capitalize the M in Man.

Many of the texts cited were not originally written in English. In several other languages, there are actually different words which translate into "man" in English but actually have different meanings in their original texts. One example is the difference in the Latin words *homo* and *vir*: both translate into "man," but the former is more properly a member of the human species while the other is an individual male. I have tried to preserve this distinction, by either capitalizing the M (as stated above), or utilizing parenthesis to indicate which use of the word "man" I am intending.

The trouble with English and genders in philosophy is exacerbated when trying to make a distinction between *a* man (vir), Man (homo), or man/woman as in a gender's nature or essence. Due to the intrinsically radical subjectivity of the human person, wide-sweeping general statements about gender run the risk of appearing egregiously inaccurate or absolutist in their stereotypical understanding of the human experience. What is true about male or female as pertains to the *nature of their gender* is not necessarily experienced the same way between human subjects, or even in some cases experienced *at all* (as in extreme cases such as gender disphoria, or even simply the varying levels of personality differences and cultural influences). The intent is to differentiate and avoid statements such as "all men/women *do* or *are* or *experience* the world this way," in favor of the more precise observation that "this particular situation or thing is *of the nature of* manhood/

womanhood, even though not all men/women may do or experience that exactly or in that particular way." It's a very tricky line to walk, but I have tried to walk it in the following manner.

Human, one individual human, or having to do with the nature of human is referred to as "Man," with a capitalized "M," as stated. "It is of the nature of Man that he is a rational creature" is an example. Man in this case = *homo*, rational animal of individual substance.

Either of the genders, considered in their own natures as abstracts (the Platonic form, if you will) and therefore necessarily without an accompanying person to embody them or experience them is referred to as "man," or "woman," in the singular and without the article *a*. I keep this in the singular because to say "men act thusly" is a generalized statement of how this particular subset of humans who *are* men behave - not that it is of the nature of the male to do thus, regardless of the human experience. "The species is complete only with the creation of both man and woman" is an example of this distinction.

Specific, individual, or personal members of the human race specifically considered as a specific human *person* (that is, an individual who experiences the world through the lens of gender as is the only possibility), is referred to as *a* man or *a* woman, again in the singular but with the accompanying article *a*. This distinction of gender as personal individuals or groups of individuals is also denoted by the plurals, "men" and "women," since the plural lends itself more to generalized statements of particular individuals rather than a thing's nature. "Kant warns of the dangers that await a man who becomes *too* enamored with women" is an example of this distinction. There is not anything *of the nature of the masculine* which necessarily follows when a male supposedly becomes too enamored with women, but the masculine gender as experienced by an individual *can* have *x* as a result of *y*.

Other minor clarifications will be made individually throughout the text.

Acknowledgments

This work contains the fingerprints of many individuals, who have knowingly or unknowingly helped me get to where I am. Some of them I am able to thank here.

First, thank you to my wife, Jacqueline Curley. I am a long winded writer, an ambitious thinker, and a hardheaded man, but somehow you are able to support and critique me through it all. Most importantly, I am your husband. Thank you for your life, and for giving context to my own.

I give thanks to my parents, James and Lori Curley. You provided that first encounter with God and freedom in an intact first community: the school of humanity you gave me as child a loving family.

Thank you to my brothers: Nick, Matthew, Thomas, and Gregory Curley. I am who I am because of you;

this book is what it is because of you. I can't imagine a world where you were not there.

Thank you to my sisters: Krystle, Theresa, and Bernadette Curley. Growing up as we did, the traditional gender roles were sometimes not as clear cut-and-dry as I would have liked them to be. You caused me to challenge my own caste mindsets, and you continue to do so. I love each of you.

Thank you to my wife's family, my in-laws: Robert, Debi, Michelle, James, Sr. Mary Brigid, OCD, Sr. Josefa, OCD, Therese, Rob, Catherine, Anne, Nicolette, and Joseph. You are a testament to the family as a school for humanity, focused on the formation of the person and beholding the value and subjectivity of the person with intrinsic value, beauty, and worth.

To my good friend, Paul Zimmermann. Professional mentor, efficient squad leader, brother in Christ and fellow Disciple. Many of these ideas have been, in one way or another, the fruits of our conversations. Though you may not agree with some of my conclusions, you have been an integral part of this book's creation. Thank you for your friendship, your iron which sharpens my own, and your intellectual honesty.

I wish to thank George Harne, John Klucinec, Peter Sampo, Mary Mumbach, Brian Fitzgerald, Joe Forte, and the rest of the faculty from Magdalen College of the Liberal Arts. The pursuit of knowledge and the importance of Leisure for a life well lived you introduced me to remains in my soul.

Thank you to my friend and mentor, Fr. Roger Boucher. Implicitly, you taught me much of what these pages contain. More directly, challenged me to think about how these and other precepts of the Faith applied to the real world.

Posthumously, and with prayers for the repose of their souls and the consolation of their families, I acknowledge my deep indebtedness to Dr. Peter Sampo and Fr. Paul Theophan, founder of Magdalen College of the Liberal Arts and Chancellor of the Melkite Eparchy of Parma, respectively. You were two of the hardest teachers I ever had, but your intense teaching style demanded a growth in me that never would have surfaced without your guidance.

I wish to thank Dr. John Hittinger and the faculty of the John Paul II Institute in the University of Saint Thomas, Houston. You introduced me to a side of Pope Saint John Paul II I would never have known. I thought I had found your program by accident; my guardian Angel intended me to find it.

Many people gave their time as beta readers, editors, and critics for this book. I thank each of you for struggling through it. You have made me a better writer; next time, I will try to emulate the style of some novelists instead of the midaevil theologians!

Introducing This Book: On Inquiries

"Logic invents as many fallacies as it detects; it is a good weapon, but as liable to be used in a bad as in a good cause." Christian Nestell Bovee, (*Day's Collacon, 1895)*

Recently, I was astounded to see a YouTube video featuring Michael Knowles entitled "Bar Fight." Of course, as anyone would do, I watched it. I, of all people, can't resist the urge to see one of my favorite commentators just open up in a fist fight. And, while that wasn't exactly what I was treated to, I was not disappointed with the *actual* production. The video was not a physical brawl; it was a heated exchange of ideas in a very public space.

If you haven't seen it yet, I do rather recommend it. There is lively participation from the other bar-goers, sound name-calling from the opposition (like every good bar fight has), and, of course, that one weirdo who somehow received the center stage for a brief moment. I never thought a bar fight would be where I find Knowles. But yet again, I was not really surprised either when I saw it published. Such theatrics are becoming more and more popular; and, rather than indicate a return of carousing and name-calling, actually herald a global return to the vicious and ultimate human sport of debate.

I will be honest: A Nashville bar would not have been one of the first places I would have looked for a publicized intellectual debate. Don't get me wrong: A beloved friend and former squad leader and I have frequented *many* bars in *several* states, wherein the beers flowed as freely as our bandied positions went back and forth. We've even made our own bar from time to time in the comfort of our own homes. And, in this, we are not alone: alcohol, friendships, and deeply personal (dare I say spiritual) conversations often go hand in hand. There is nothing like the moderate shared drink to establish some camaraderie and loosen the tongue just a bit. So, though I found myself surprised at finding *Knowles* featured in a Nashville bar, the simple fact that there was a discussion happening and being videoed in a bar was not *that* surprising.

The debate itself did not surprise me. What did surprise me, however, was the public nature of the debate, the ground rules surrounding it, and the public figures participating. It was a formal affair, complete with microphones, voting, and some level of moderation. Now, that is not to say it did not devolve into insults, weird topics, and even weirder audience participation: It just wouldn't have been a bar fight without all the rest. No, it was an honest-to-goodness fight, just not with fists. It was a fight of ideas and words. And the audience loved it.

The most surprising thing about the whole affair was how *into it* the audience got. They bought it, hook, line, and sinker. And, judging by the decibel levels from the crowd, Knowles wasn't even unanimously agreed with—even though Nashville is his own turf. Some of the other ideas were looked upon favorably by the cheering (and booing) audience as well. And even though there was a clear loser in the fight, even *his* ideas were met with interest from some parties. All this to say: The public exchange of ideas was enthralling enough in a bar to merit active participation and to avoid calls to turn the TV back on.

The sport of public debate is back. It has been on the rise for quite some time. The world simply is not capable of operating under the radical subjectivity we have been subjected to in the past decades. People are increasingly interested in watching Knowles debate, taking classes from the Crucible and Andrew Wilson, seeing Charlie Kirk (requiescat in pace) collide with college campus, and so many more.

The return of the sport of debate allows us to witness, experience, and participate in something once commonplace in the great societies of history. And yet, even as discourse is returning to our everyday lives as the medium of truth-seekers, its existence in the public sphere is merely tenuous. While popular platforms, such as Jubilee, allow for a lot of good sound bites and might trick us into thinking that a debate is happening, there is no true exchange of ideas there. Ideas clashing and contrasting in the eyes of the viewer isn't really a debate, nor is it a conversation between two parties. Rather, too often modern "debate" platforms allow for two people to talk right past each other, insult each other, and walk away feeling superior. What is lacking is an engagement with both opposing parties in a way that is simultaneously coherent in its worldview, willing to hear the opposing worldviews, and seeks to uncover the truth in a way that might be known. And so, the continued presence of a *true* debate relies on how we as a society can answer two questions: *What does it mean to be "open-minded?"* and *What does it mean to "know" something, anything?*

The first question, What does it mean to be open-minded?, is the prerequisite for all good-faith discussion. We begin every position from an opinion supposed to be true: No one personally holds a stance they think is *wrong* or absurd. A person may play devil's advocate, engage in sophistry, intentionally mislead, or simply reject discourse in his stubborn attempts at "winning." But every position we genuinely hold as true (including the timidity that causes us to end our advice with, "I don't know, though . . ."), we hold only because we think it is actually *right*. If we did not think it was correct, we would simply be incapable of holding it as our own.

And yet, with the return of debate as a public sport, we find ourselves confronted with the clash of ideas in the open marketplace—and the opportunity to confront different beliefs from our own. How do we know whether we are right or wrong in our own opinions? We are in the precarious state of trying to hold *some* stable notions so that we are not mere driftwood people, and yet not hold our own opinions *so* true that we are the arbiters and ultimate judges of what is correct and what is false. Under this light, the question about what it means to be "open-minded" now becomes: *How is it that I come to truly* know *about anything—including myself?* And *that* is the first question I intend to address in this book.

The second question, on the nature of the verb *to know*, is clearly related to the first question. If we hold something to be true, then there must be some basis or metric by which we are able to judge its validity, value, and verifiability. But how are we to know that what I hold to be true is not merely my opinion? Since I have subjective senses, and everyone comes at the same object from different perspectives, how am I to know that I am right, and another's genuinely held position is simply wrong? We have already stated that we must begin from a place of stability in order to actually reach traction in a conversation: *Where do we find that stability from which to proceed?* This is the second question I intend to address in this book.

In short, *both* questions can be answered with the same statement: There is an objective truth, and that Truth is *personal* in nature. It is not simply true that *we, persons*, encounter truth as subjective individuals with senses, opinions, and backgrounds; it is also true that the truth is a *Person* who beckons us come, recognize Him in the created nature we perceive around us.

It is true: We encounter the world and formulate opinions based on the data we receive through our senses. The data collected and interpreted by us is as unique and numerous as there are people on the earth. But if we left our considerations at that concession of subjectivity (as so many institutions of higher learning do today), we end up with a sort of radical relativism that leaves us free to accept or dismiss another's statement as "your truth." It is as absurd in the grand scheme of things as it is insurmountable to the individual arrested in this thought who goes no further.

This precarious and at times humorous predicament is captured beautifully by Chesterton in his book, *Orthodoxy*. There, he describes insanity (or, in our case, the absurdity of relativism) as somewhat beautiful—but recognizable or beautiful only in relation to and by the not-insane (or through objective truth). He writes:

> It is true that some speak lightly and loosely of insanity as in itself attractive. But a moment's thought will show that if disease is beautiful, it is generally someone else's disease. A blind man may be picturesque; but it requires two eyes to see the picture. And similarly even the wildest poetry of insanity can only be enjoyed by the sane. To the insane man his insanity is quite prosaic, because it is quite true. A man who thinks himself a chicken is to himself as ordinary as a chicken. A man who thinks he is a bit of glass is to himself as dull as a bit of glass. It is the homogeneity of his mind which makes him dull, and which makes him mad. It is only because we see the irony of his idea that we think him even amusing; it is only because he does not see the irony of his idea that he is put in Hanwell at all. In short, oddities only strike ordinary people. Oddities do not strike odd people.[1]

For the person arrested in their own subjectivity, their worldview is complete. They are content to hold the truth as mere point of view, as perception based on cultural construct and sense receptivity. And hopefully, by reading this book, you will know how to refute that

1. G. K. Chesterton, *Orthodoxy* (New York, NY: Barnes & Noble, 2007), 8.

absurdity—and realize how we got to suppose it true in the first place.

The Intended Audience for This Book

Any good writer, publisher, beta reader, or editor is bound to approach the project at hand with one primary question in mind: *Who is the intended audience?* I *know* they approach it this way because it has been the universal initial reaction I have received. This being the case, I do not think I am a very good writer.

My military career has taught me that a sentence is only allowed a maximum of fifteen words, that only the active voice is used, and that you must maintain professionalism and conciseness at all costs. Conversely, academia taught me to write so that my readers' interest is kept and engaged. In addition, I am encouraged to write utilizing stories and examples to encourage my readers' memory and understanding of the topics at hand. I am free to use the passive voice. Finally, I am able to engage with hard, abstract concepts in the spirit of dialogue and exploration. A good writer would take both of these styles and combine them to create a work that concisely communicates concepts while also providing a presentation worthy of a painter. I apparently combine the two into an amalgam that leaves many scratching their heads at its density and confusing presentation. It turns out that *I* am my own primary intended audience.

If you are like me, welcome to this book. You are a Catholic (or at least an active Christian) whose faith plays a consequential role in your decision-making and worldview. Personal freedom is important to you, as is upholding the dignity and freedom of the person (whatever that means). You see the world progressing toward chaos and Western society progressing toward an increasingly isolationist foundation. You consider yourself an ideological moderate, rather than extreme on one side or the other. You lament society's decreasing orientation toward autonomous license and away from coherent cooperation. You wonder (or are interested in) how we got to this chaotic society and wonder if the path to sanity is in our rearview mirror or lies ahead of us. Finally, you enjoy open-minded discussions and are willing to follow them wherever they may lead—even if that road is twisty at times. If this is you, you are in for a treat.

If the above description is *not* you, don't worry. You are also welcomed with excited enthusiasm. Though some of the concepts within this book are presented with technical language, I firmly believe the discussion held within these pages is accessible to anyone who seeks to engage. If you find yourself with little to no philosophical background, those technical subtleties may prove harder to grasp at first read. I would encourage you to do two things.

First, I encourage you to read slowly and find someone with whom to discuss what you read. Knowledge and understanding are intricately linked with being able to discuss that which we consume. And second, seek additional context for some points of discussion. For a coherent progression of thought, I tend to give a brief overview of where such figures as Plato, Aristotle, Kant, Ratzinger, and Pieper (to name a few) fall on the particular issue I am discussing. If this is your first time hearing any of these names, or you have not read any of their primary sources, I encourage you to spend some time getting to know those authors. Though the overview I give to each key author is accurate to my understanding, it remains a gross oversimplification of the author's worldview. These brief summations do a disservice to the authors unless you are already familiar with them.

Now that you know who the book is for and what it is about, I would like to give you a brief overview of our conversation to come. Hopefully, the summation I present to you here will serve as a roadmap of sorts to return to. If I am successful, it will provide you with contextual relevancy for where our discussion is headed and where we have come from.

Overview of the Argument

The foundational principles of our discussion are epistemology, teleology, *anamnesis* (commonly—if not strictly accurately—called *conscience*), personhood, freedom, will, and desire. Both in a spirit of discussion and in an attempt to retrace how we got to our current societal premises, we try to move in a linear fashion, from classical philosophy through modernity. In short, we hopefully encapsulate where we are in society today and where we go from here.

Our first stop is establishing a connection between knowledge and the body. This is achieved through closely related Chapters I and II: They focus on how the *person* is related to the *body* by briefly exploring the science of *epistemology*, or the study of how and what we can know. Our discussion surrounding the necessity of the body for knowledge and action will move from epistemology proper to the subcategory of teleology. *Teleology* is the study of what we can know about a thing by its ends, or purposes. Here, we take as a given that God exists.[2] Through the created reality, God reveals Himself to the person by way of encounter through a recognition of the moral order. The moral order itself is experienced in the physical world through the body and recognized by the dictates of conscience.

---

2. Knowing who this book is for, such an assumption is appropriate and warranted. Taking God's existence as a given does come with certain extending ramifications beyond simply that He is an entity, however. For the Christian, God existing necessitates that He is the Creator, He is Spirit, etc. Not all of these assumptions will be taken specifically as given, and we will deal with certain attributes of God and their proofs as appropriate. This being said, it is worthwhile to note that here, at the beginning of our discussion, we take the Christian God to exist and therefore be of consequence in our reasoning.

Our discussion will claim that *conscience*, not *consciousness*, is the defining point of personhood and subjectivity in human experience through the senses. A properly formed conscience orients us to see the world in terms of an encounter with God, created to bring us closer to Him—even though the dictates of conscience are often not such a formal recognition of God. We will also see that utilizing conscience as a defining point of personhood necessitates an inclination toward community with other persons. Human inclination toward a community of persons leads us to the conclusion that the male body is unintelligible without reference to the female body, and vice versa.

In both Chapters I and II, we touch upon an important ramification of assuming the Christian God exists: He is our Creator. As an Intelligent Being, God creates only with a specific end in mind. Every created reality has an end or purpose, which is essential to its nature and makeup. As a result, we will conclude that the gendered body matters as a way of encountering God through the physical world. The gendered body must have a specific purpose within the physical world, informing the person how they are to act toward other persons as they seek to fulfill their innate inclination toward community. Through the course of Chapters I and II, we discuss *epistemology* (how and what we know), *teleology* (knowing things according to their purpose), and *anamnesis. Anamnesis* is a technical term in Christian writing coined by Cardinal

Ratzinger as a specific way of speaking of the conscience. Though these topics may seem an abstract technical beginning, they constitute a necessary part of our larger discussion.

Introduced through Chapters I and II, our discussion of *anamnesis* continues in Chapter III. Utilizing the writings of Cardinal Ratzinger, we discuss how anamnesis within the soul is aware of God, even if only subconsciously. It orients the person toward Him through a recognition upon encounter. This primal awareness of God stems from knowledge of the divine, which has been instilled into the heart of Man from the moment of the person's creation. Conscience demands the human person seek and encounter the truth about God in the physical world, orienting the actor toward constantly choosing God as the Chief Good[3] which truly makes Man happy. As a result, it will follow that freedom is an essential characteristic of the person, and an attribute which must always be championed and protected. What is more, acting through freedom in the pursuit of adhering to conscience allows the individual to actually know themselves and be more in touch with their own identity, since they will be engaging in activity that is already present within themselves as those specific ways they encounter God.

---

3. Though we discuss *briefly* how God's existence necessitates His goodness, this attribute, too, is largely held as appropriately assumed.

We continue in Chapter III to address the grave confusion regarding the nature of freedom today, present as one of the central dilemmas in society and a key component to the equality paradox. This confusion stems from misconceptions of freedom, construed as an *autonomous license*—a capacity not to choose to pursue what brings us happiness but rather to decide whether we wish to pursue happiness or evil. These misconceptions are inherited from the philosophies of modernity, particularly evident in the writings of William of Ockham. The idea that one is more free only insofar as he is able to choose without external influence contradicts our concept of personhood through the conscience. The claim of conscience is that God Himself, a Person external to the human subject, has placed this inner orientation toward the good within the heart of the person. The correct understanding of the freedom found within the human person and how it relates to Man as a body-soul composite endowed with reason is the concluding topic of this chapter.

Concluding the Introduction

Michael Knowles is no small figure within the public sphere. He has more than just a Wikipedia page. He has testified to Congress. He has a very successful show. He is an actor, comedian, cigar salesman, and debater. And yet, to hear him speak, one is not subjected to an egoism born from a sort of elitism in exclusively being right: Knowles, *in spite* of his correct positions, bears himself with a sort of humility and levity that is as disarming as it is remarkable.

Now, this book is most assuredly *not* a fan book about Knowles. He simply serves as a very proximate example of someone who successfully applies a virtue long known to be foundational to basic human activity: humility. Everything we do—debate, discern our personal preferences, create culture, everything—must first come from a place of humility. We must cultivate a sense of vulnerability and openness to a truth that lies outside our personal bubble, if we are ever to proceed along the road to knowledge.

One might think that our world today is simply bereft of humility. We certainly do not see openness, vulnerability, and good-faith discussions happening, even as we see a rise in debate within the public sphere. It might seem that the world no longer has humility might be a fair conclusion. I, however, agree with Chesterton when he offers an alternate view.

Again, turning to *Orthodoxy*, we find Chesterton suggesting there is not so much an *absence* of humility in the world as much as there is a *misplaced* humility. He writes:

> Modesty has moved from the organ of ambition. Modesty has settled upon the organ of conviction; where it was never meant to be. A man was meant to be doubtful about himself, but undoubting about the truth; this has been

> exactly reversed. Nowadays the part of a man that a man does assert is exactly the part he ought not to assert—himself. The part he doubts is exactly the part he ought not to doubt—the Divine Reason . . . we are on the road to producing a race of men too mentally modest to believe in the multiplication table. We are in danger of seeing philosophers who doubt the law of gravity as being a mere fancy of their own.[4]

Humility with regard to oneself is simply paramount to any knowledge or exchange of ideas. When the truth is personal, we are tasked with not so much cataloguing data as much as we are learning what that person reveals about themselves. We reveal *ourselves* to that person in response.

And so, with no small amount of humility, I welcome you to the discussion contained within the book that follows. There are not many (if any) original ideas that you will find herein; I, like so many before me, stand on the shoulders of Giants, and relate other authors' works to my own musings.

And yet, though you may not find *originality* in the pages that come after, you may find a unique perspective in how they relate to each other. If nothing else, I hope you will find them to be a roadmap which can lead back to a correct anthropological understanding of Man's epistemology. From that foundational

---

4. Chesterton, *Orthodoxy*, 24.

understanding of Man, the operations of his intellect, the nature of Truth, and Man's freedom in relation to that Truth, I hope my esteemed readers will find themselves well-equipped to take their place behind the microphone. Enter into the public sphere of debate! Boldly defend yourselves in the open marketplace of ideas! And, above all, I hope and encourage you to find yourselves as willing participants in a life aligned with knowledge of the Truth.

Let us begin.

CHAPTER I

Knowledge

"At times I feel certain I am right while not knowing the reason. When the eclipse of 1919 confirmed my intuition... I would have been astonished had it turned out otherwise. Imagination is more important than knowledge. For knowledge is limited, whereas imagination embraces the entire world, stimulating progress, giving birth to evolution. It is, strictly speaking, a real factor in scientific research." Albert Einstein, (*Cosmic Religion and Other Opinions and Aphorisms, 1931*)

O*edipus Rex,* a timeless classic tragedy from the annals of history, serves as the introduction to our discussion. There are many great topics to contemplate and discuss in this Greek tragedy. While discussions associated with it frequently revolve around the study of apparently self-fulfilling prophecies, our purpose causes us to examine *Oedipus Rex* with a focus on knowledge and Man's search for truth. A brief recap of the narrative will set us off on the right path.

***

A plague hangs over the ancient city of Thebes. The citizens cry out to their king to save them, he who has saved them from curses before. Oedipus, the noble leader and lover of his people, sends his priest to visit the oracle to beg for insight into how he might rid the city of disaster. The priest returns, claiming the plague will cease only when the murderer of Oedipus's predecessor, Laius, is brought to justice. Believing this to be a simple enough task and just in its own right, Oedipus starts investigating the murder immediately. He summons the blind prophet Tiresias to divine the killer's identity.

Tiresias enters as summoned but is reluctant to answer any specific questions about the matter at hand. A senator implores him, "If thou hast knowledge, do not turn away, When all of us implore thee suppliant!"

to which Tiresias replies, "Ye, Are all unknowing . . . I will not say, lest I display thy sorrow."[5] Oedipus becomes enraged and threatens the prophet, who names Oedipus himself as the murderer. Tiresias cryptically continues, saying that Oedipus is standing in shame and living with those closest to him. He becomes explicit: "And since you have reproached me with my blindness, I say—you have your sight, and do not see What evils are about you, nor with whom, Nor in what home you are dwelling."[6]

The plight of Oedipus increases throughout the story from that point onward. As he hears a similar prophecy told to his wife, we witness the long dawning of realization in Oedipus's mind that the story of Laius's murder aligns with a story he himself tells from the antagonist's view. Through these events, we can only find ourselves agreeing with Tiresias: that ignorance of this prophecy would indeed be bliss. Oedipus cannot help himself once his quest for knowledge has begun, even when his wife/mother, Jocasta, recognizes the truth before him and begs him to be content. Oedipus proclaims, "I will not hearken—not to know the whole."[7] His quest for knowledge results in tragedy, just as Tiresias indicated it would. Realizing at last that *he* is

---

5. Sophocles, *Oedipus Rex*, trans. Sir George Young (Mineola, NY: Dover Publications, 2012), scene I, Apple Books.
6. Sophocles, *Oedipus Rex,* sc. I.
7. Sophocles, *Oedipus Rex*, sc. III.

his father's murderer and has married his own mother—in good faith though it be—he exiles and blinds himself. Jocasta completes the tragedy by taking her own life in her shame.

***

We can see a peculiar tendency in Oedipus throughout the play. He is given ample time and many opportunities to turn back from his investigation into Laius's murder. He is even given an opportunity to save Thebes *and* his dignity by "exiling" himself, in a sense, by becoming king of Corinth instead. Nevertheless, Oedipus persists in demanding to hear the testimonies of those who know the truth, to his own horror. In spite of his opportunities for life and happily ever after, Oedipus cannot help but seek out the truth of the incident—and his origins. His tenacious attraction toward the truth illustrates the observation Aristotle would proclaim many years later: that at our core, "All Men [human beings] by nature desire to know."[8]

History bears witness to knowledge as an innate human desire. Every work passed down to our own day echoes this sentiment, either explicitly or implicitly. Modern-day science, the rapid increase in technological advances, and the various theories articulated to

8. Aristotle, *Metaphysics,* in *The Basic Works of Aristotle*, ed. Richard McKeon (New York, New York: Modern Library, 2001), book A (I), 980a, Kindle.

explain the cosmos are born of Man's intrinsic orientation to search for the truth. It is not enough that Man *has* reason and cognitive powers—he has the burning desire to *use* these faculties. It is not simply a matter that he *can*; in a sense, he *must*.

The story of Oedipus suggests more than Man desires truth, however. It intimates that there is one particular *kind* of truth that he searches for. Man does not seek to acquire knowledge as so many facts that can be categorized and logged. Oedipus himself had *all* the information and context he needed to see the whole from his original conversation with Tiresias. Nonetheless, he remains oblivious to the horrific truth until he hears it in a specific manner that resonates with his mind's eye, causing him to *recognize* the truth. This tragedy illustrates that Man utilizes his reason not only to *uncover facts* so that he may logically progress from one valid premise to another but also to reach a culminating experience and encounter with the *whole* of reality.

The encounter with the truth Oedipus experienced, that all-encompassing *recognition*, is the same encounter all Men seek. It is often described as a dawning realization of understanding, not merely seeing each individual part of the reasoning process. In one sense, we can conclude from this that there are *two* types of knowledge sought: the factual, data-driven knowledge of the categorizable on the one hand and the freer, *understanding*-based knowledge of all the parts working together in their proper context within reality.

Our reflection on knowledge as seen in *Oedipus Rex* leaves us with the question: *How can we say that we* know, *and exactly* what *is it that we can know?* This question is the subject of the science known as *epistemology.*

The "World" of Man: What Can We Know?

Man has historically regarded the world with a sense of wonder. Many of his attempts to explain the encounterable cosmos stem from this world of wonderment. He created mythical gods and creatures as explanations or metaphors for understanding creation. Later on, he developed, more specifically, data-driven sciences to explain the coming of the seasons and the physical world around him, examining even the moon and stars. Of particular interest to Man has been his own self-discovery: both the nature of his own existence and why, in the course of human events, he must eventually die.

Throughout history, Man has accepted the data received through his senses and has tried to account for what he has received by positing theories. Through time, reason and means of observation progress. As a consequence, individual theories, as attempts to explain observed reality, cease to adequately explain truth and appear false. When this happens, Man cannot rest until he has again found some new and, at least, apparently true explanation to pacify his searching mind. Ptolemy, for example, developed his explanations in astronomy in a specific way in order to preserve the preconceived belief in the heavens as making up the heavenly spheres. His model of the solar system placed the *Earth* as the center of the cosmos, and the Ptolemaic geocentric astronomy model was born. Contrast this with Copernicus, who years later abandoned the perfectly functional Ptolemaic system to develop his own account of the celestial phenomena. His starting premise? Developing a solar system model that would appropriately reflect a design by the Christian God. For those who believe in divine revelation, God is the most Perfect Craftsman. He simply would not make such a monstrous and complex cosmos as was explained by Ptolemy's model. Thus, through reasoning in light of the Christian God as a consequential fact to be considered, the first operable heliocentric solar system model was constructed.[9]

Man's reason contemplates everything he encounters or experiences in the world. Through beholding things as they are, he finds himself increasingly more capable of deeper and wider contemplation, seemingly without end. The continual contemplation of the cosmos causes Man to behold deeper and more complete realities; in exercising his reason, he finds his own "'living area' . . . broadened and raised up to the supernatural level of divine life. Man lives in God and by God: he lives 'according to the Spirit,' and 'sets his

---

9. There is an intrinsic link between science (the formal discipline as understood today), philosophy, and theology that we would be remiss not to point out. In short, these three disciplines can never *truly* be separated. As an illustration of the integral connection between these three, consider the progression of astronomy. Barring satellite imagery, the Ptolemaic system is *still* an operable model of the solar system and, in some aspects, actually explains how the cosmos works *better* than the currently held theory of the sun as the center. But, in light of revelation and our knowledge of how *ordered* the cosmos is, the Ptolemaic system seems out of place. If God exists, He must be accounted for (that is to say, even on a philosophical level, a geocentric solar system makes no sense in light of theology).

We cannot pretend, at every stage of thought, to start from scratch—nor can we fully suspend theological discussions as if they were of no account. Scientists do not do as much, nor do theologians. Because of this, while this book claims to be primarily a philosophical project, it really has overtones of both scientific inquiry and theological foundation as well.

mind on the things of the Spirit.'"[10] This much to say, Man's reason is designed to contemplate the world not simply as abstract, cataloging facts for facts' own sake. Rather, Man is designed to encounter reality as both a physical and a spiritual being, to contemplate "everything that is,"[11] and to exist in "the whole of reality."[12]

To claim that Man is called, let alone capable, of contemplating the *whole of reality* is a bold claim. At first blush, it seems almost certain to go too far. The objection might be raised: Surely man is a *finite* being with limited capability of reason! Nevertheless, we make this claim here boldly and in earnest. The paradoxical limitations of Man's reason and his capacity for contemplative thought on every subject, in reality, is one of the greatest mysteries of the nature of Man—and one of the classical proofs for the immortality of the soul. In order to understand this, we must make a brief distinction between knowledge as a possession of fact versus knowledge as a form of contemplating the whole. Put simply, one is a stagnant logging of facts (as if everything in the cosmos was quantifiable with the same surety), while the other is a humble reflection.

---

10. John Paul II, *Dominum et Vivificantem* (Vatican City: Vatican Press, 1986), paragraph 8.

11. Aristotle, *De Anima,* in *The Basic Works of Aristotle,* ed. Richard McKeon (New York, New York: Modern Library, 2001), book I, chapter 5, 409b.

12. Josef Pieper, *Leisure: The Basis of Culture,* Including *The Philosophical Act* (San Francisco, CA: Ignatius Press, 2009), 99.

The requirement for the latter is a constant development of man's contemplative attitude toward creation, engaging in exercises aimed at widening the world that man perceives so that further and deeper contemplation is possible. Let us take, for example, a *crow's* world of perception. Incapable of rational thought, a crow observes the raw, isolated datum that surrounds him—without context or reference to the whole. So incapable is the crow of contemplation that he is:

> Utterly unable to see a grasshopper that is not moving . . . We are perhaps inclined to suppose that although the shape of the grasshopper is familiar to the crow, it is unable to recognize a grasshopper if a blade of grass cuts across it, it cannot recognize the "unity" grasshopper—just as we find it quite difficult to recognize a familiar object in a picture puzzle. On this assumption it is only when the grasshopper jumps that its shape becomes recognizable and dissociates itself from the surrounding images . . . if [an insect's] motionless form simply does not exist in the field of vision of their enemies, then by shamming death they drop out of that world with absolute certainty and cannot be found even though searched for.[13]

Captured as he is in a world of mere instinct and sensory registration, the crow is even incapable of

13. Pieper, *Leisure*, 96.

recognizing that which is most beneficial to him: a juicy grasshopper dinner. A grasshopper simply does not *exist* in the crow's world.

Unlike the crow's limited world, the *world* of Man, so to speak, is *all of reality*. This much to say, his mind is designed to *behold*, not simply register. He is capable of looking at reality with the sense of unity appropriate to an intelligible cosmos, but only if he continually increases his own world. When Man does not exercise himself through his mind, widening his field of vision and aiming with humility at knowledge of the highest things, the eye of his mind imitates the eye of the crow. He becomes unable to distinguish between the isolated datum that surrounds him and the cohesive unity of the cosmos. In such a Man, some aspect or another of reality is, therefore, necessarily *outside* of his world, though he looks for it and could encounter it right in front of him.

The crux of the claim here is one of *disposition toward the whole of reality.* Instead of *a conquering or owning reality through categorical logging of fact,* it is a "listening to the essence of things."[14] In this light, we can accurately say that there is nothing that exists such that it cannot be considered, contemplated, and reflected upon in the mind of Man. Even the most impossible mystery known to Man, the concept of the Blessed Trinity, exists within his world: He can behold the Trinity in his mind and can contemplate this great

14. Pieper, *Leisure*, 28.

mystery.[15] Contemplation itself thus becomes a source of knowledge for Man.

Through his rational power, Man exists as a union between physical realities and the spiritual world; as such, he is not merely in pursuit of the truth concerning the physical realm. Man does not seek knowledge *of* something but rather *knowledge itself.* The knowledge he seeks, in its pure, unadulterated form, envelops all truth. Man exists through his reason in "'the' world in

---

15. A disclaimer is required here. The truth and fullness of the Blessed Trinity, understood as Three Persons in One God, is most certainly a matter of revelation and cannot be detected by Man. It is neither a matter of pragmatic knowledge nor can it be *comprehended* by Man. Nonetheless, that it *has* been revealed illustrates that there is nothing in the cosmos that Man *cannot* know, even if he needs some help to see it. Contrast this to the crow, who can literally be shown the unmoving grasshopper but still not observe it. While the crow cannot receive revelation, Man can be shown that which he cannot detect, and it becomes part of his world. The unmoving grasshopper will *never* be a part of the crow's world, even if he is shown it explicitly.

In this, too, we see another example of the intricate link between theology and philosophy. Though he fell far short of recognizing or even conceiving of the Trinity as such, pagan philosopher Aristotle, centuries before Christ, reasoned not only that one God exists but that He exists *in community*. Though Man would need divine revelation to truly know God as Three Persons in community with Himself, Aristotle demonstrated an innate *disposition* towards even revealed truths—though not superseding or rendering revelation unnecessary.

the sense of *visibilia omnia et invisibilia*," the world which encompasses "the whole of reality."

Man's knowledge does not *encompass* all of reality and truth but rather dwells *within its sphere*. There is a subtle distinction here. One position says Man "takes himself up into the center of his own unity and [is made] one spirit with God [and in this spirit] stands ahead of all things."[16] The other posits that Man merely perceives what really exists to the extent to which he is capable.

Within the sphere of "the whole of reality," the soul has "seen all things that there are [and so, has] knowledge of them all . . . the soul has learned all things."[17] This is not to mean that the soul already contains within itself all facts about reality in the sense of *scientific data,* per se. Rather, it is a sense of *recognizing reality* or *encountering it*. What is meant here is that the sphere of Man is beholding and recognizing the thing as it really is in all its fullness—not the ability to recite all the specific categorizable details about an object. This distinction of *encompassing* versus *existing* within the sphere of the whole of reality is, though indeed subtle, of no little importance. *Encompassing* denotes a level of conquest and categorization; *existing* denotes

---

16. Giovanni Pico Della Mirandola, *On the Dignity of Man* (Indianapolis, IN: Hackett Publishing Company, 1998), 5.
17. Plato, *Meno,* in *The Essential Plato*, trans. Benjamin Jowett and M. J. Knight (New York, NY: Quality Paperback Book Club, 1999), 443.

a level of active contemplation and beholding of that which exists outside of yourself in marvel and wonder.

How We Think About Reality

Many thinkers throughout history have developed theories on how Man engages with the world around him. Indeed, any discussion on epistemology must properly include Plato's theory of *recollection*, and one might be surprised that we jump directly to Aquinas's embrace of Aristotelian epistemology. If you have never heard of Plato before, you will not notice his absence. For those familiar with his dialogues, never fear: Plato and his recollection will return before the end of our chapter. For now, we must refrain from exploring the entire history of epistemology as such, restricting ourselves only to what is expedient and directly related to where we are, how we got here, and where the truth lies. We shall accept much of the school Aquinas fell into concerning teleology and use him as our functional base. Eventually, we will discuss the counter-epistemology of modernity and the Enlightenment as prevailing work foundational to the inherited errors of our own day.

Aquinas holds a holistic view of Man's encounter with the created world. For Aquinas, as was for Aristotle before him, the primary principle of human reason is that all knowledge first comes through the senses. The will follows by acting toward what it deems good according to the knowledge gained through the senses. The mind accepts the experienced reality, whereupon the imaginative and estimative powers begin to abstract and interpret. Finally, the memory weighs the experience against other prior experiences, allowing the intellect to make a final determination and interpretation on the merit of the experience and a course of action. From these principles, we conclude that Man relies completely on his senses to give him knowledge of the world.[18]

For the most part, Aquinas holds that we can rely on our senses to give us reliable information, categorizing this information and knowing an object through contemplation of that object's *causes* and by its movement from potency to act. Though we can determine four

---

18. This is a very technical and brief summation of how Aquinas describes the soul's rational operation. We will return to a detailed exploration of this, complete with helpful examples, in Chapter II.

distinct causes for everything—efficient, material, formal, and final, Aristotelian (and therefore Thomistic) epistemology reminds us that it is primarily through a thing's *final* cause that we are able to determine exactly what it is. Aristotle writes, "Knowledge is the object of our inquiry, and men do not think they know a thing till they have grasped the 'why' of it (which is to grasp its primary cause)."[19] The *final cause* is the sense of end, or "that for the sake of which a thing is done."[20] From this final cause springs forth all the other causes, why and in what way it moves from a state of potency to act, and the very essence of the thing itself.

The final cause gives us the necessary information we need to determine basic knowledge about a thing. We can know the object's *form* and *telos,* its *nature* and *end.* Knowledge of the cosmos through the understanding that things have a form and a telos is called *teleology.* More specifically, *teleology* is the understanding of an object by its end. By understanding the *end* (or *telos,* purpose) of any individual thing, derived by observing the *form* of the object (the appearances, design, maker, etc., of the object in question), we may understand something more about the nature of the thing itself.

---

19. Aristotle, *Physics,* in *The Basic Works of Aristotle,* ed. Richard McKeon (New York, New York: Modern Library, 2001), book II, chapter 3, 194b.
20. Aristotle, *Physics,* 194b.

Forms and telos deal with the respective truth and goodness of an object. They provide knowledge of what an object is and how it exists and performs in the context of the world. A watch, for example, has the end of keeping and communicating the present time to whoever consults it. We determine this by observing the features that make up the object we call *watch,* looking into manufacturers, and looking at what the watch is made of. Knowing that timekeeping/communicating is the end of a watch allows us to make determinations about the nature of the *watch* in general, as well as come to conclusions about a particular watch we are encountering. From factual observations such as, "'This watch is grossly inaccurate and irregular in time keeping' and 'this watch is too heavy to carry about comfortably,' the evaluative conclusion validly follows that 'this is a *bad* watch.'"[21]

From an *"is"* premise, simply observing *what* and *how* a thing is, we are able (in classical philosophy) to derive an *"ought"* conclusion, a moral or evaluative judgment of a thing based on its existence. Our encounter with one particular watch—whose end is the keeping of time—grants us some knowledge of *watches in general*. We can extend our understanding of a watch beyond this particular instance and see certain things that must be true of *all watches*. What is

---

21. Alasdair MacIntyre, *After Virtue: A Study in Moral Theory,* 3rd ed. (Notre Dame, IN: University of Notre Dame Press, 2007), 57–58.

more, there is intrinsic to the concept of watch a certain judgement appropriately applied to each individual object. Knowing the end of a watch suggests that "the concept of watch cannot be defined independently of the concept of a *good* watch . . . and that the criterion of something's being a watch and the criterion for something's being a good watch are not independent of each other."[22] Thus, we can both determine that a good watch behaves in *x* manner and that this particular watch is either good or bad because it behaves in *y* manner.

Just as we can speak of a watch through contemplation of its end, so too can we come to the knowledge of the nature of Man through his end. The end of Man, classically understood, is "having an essential nature and an essential purpose or function . . . to fill a set of roles, each of which has its own point and purpose: member of a family, citizen, soldier, philosopher, servant of God."[23] If we accept this as true, we then know something about Man both as a species and as a particular individual. We can determine what defects must be remedied or have already been remedied in order to make a *good* individual Man by measuring it up with the teleology of his being.

Understanding forms and ends stabilizes language and gives meaning to the sounds we utter, not as ideas themselves but as forms communicating the

22. MacIntyre, *After Virtue*, 58.
23. MacIntyre, *After Virtue*, 59.

idea in the speaker. To be sure, there is some concession (or assumption) that an external, detectable reality exists as a starting requirement to understand the world through terms of forms and telos. You have to admit the relative accuracy of your own senses in experiencing the world as a bare minimum for gathering accurate data. Classical philosophers had sufficient personal security in their own thought to rely on their sensory data and could come to a state of knowledge that *beheld* the world as it was. Their conclusions were not reduced to a categorized view of the world into so many little, isolated facts.

Dialectic

Though observing facts was a necessary component and often the precursor of beholding the whole, a simple catalog of these facts was never the end goal of philosophical discourse. The goal was always a full, contextualized knowledge through contemplating the whole. The all-encompassing, encountering form of knowledge is known as *intellectus;* the geometric, fact-listing, categorizing form of knowledge is known as *ratio.*

Ratio

German Philosopher Josef Pieper, in his book *The Philosophical Act*, describes *ratio* as "the power of discursive, logical thought, of searching and examination, of abstraction, of definition, and drawing conclusions."[24] Many moderns consider it to be concrete knowledge or even the only true knowledge. An example of *ratio* would be the logical steps followed in a geometrical proposition or the deduction of a detective at a crime scene. Mathematics of all kinds are an excellent example of *ratio* since there is in this discipline a sort of "certainty [in the] evidence of its reasonings," developing foundations which are "so solid and firm"[25] that they cannot be refuted. *Ratio* is clearly seen in geometry and the sciences, which are based firmly on discursive reasoning and depend so heavily upon the concreteness of measurable fact.

Ratio as a form of reasoning has always been considered a form of work, a consideration validated by our own experience. It is necessary, for sure knowledge "is certainly quite impossible without work, without the *labor improbus* of discursive thought."[26] *Ratio* is the *act* of reasoning, properly understood as moving from premise to conclusion, based on a series of logical arguments and observations. As such, *ratio* is "the properly human element in our knowledge."[27]

Ratio's intrinsically active, documenting, and categorical nature leading toward fuller understanding is described in Plato's *Republic* through the man

---

24. Pieper, *Leisure*, 28.
25. René Descartes, *Discourse on Method and Meditations on First Philosophy,* 4th ed., trans. Donald A. Cress (Indianapolis, IN: Hackett Publishing Company, 1998), 5.
26. Pieper, *Leisure*, 30.
27. Pieper, *Leisure,* 28.

who, freed from the cave, can at first "see the shadows best . . . and then the objects themselves; then he will gaze upon the light of the moon and the stars and the spangled heaven; and he will see the sky and the stars by night better than the sun or the light of the sun by day."[28] *Ratio* is primarily concerned with the measurable world. It finds its strength in categorizing and perceiving the visible realm, which ancient philosophy thought was unintelligible by itself. For all its strengths and necessity, however, *ratio* does not, on its own, progress into the full, teleological knowledge his mind desires.

Ratio is not its own end. By itself, *ratio* remains incomplete. Its primary goal is to lead the intellect of Man toward something external to itself. The results of *ratio* can sometimes be reached through shortcuts, using technology such as calculators to do the "work" part for us, but even then, we are reliant on the accuracy of the data input into the technology and then trust the result given. In no way can we consider this to be an understanding of the whole, simply as a consequence of completing the work of the problem. Something else is needed.

Intellectus

Man's knowledge is not purely rooted in the physical, nor is he content with mere categorization of

---

28. Plato, *The Republic,* 267.

the material world; through contemplation, he rather "reaches out beyond the sphere of the 'human,' touching on the order of pure spirits."[29] This is the knowledge which *ratio* is geared toward, the culminating experience which completes it. This transcendent knowledge is called *intellectus. Intellectus is true* "understanding" in so far as it is the capacity of *simplex intuitus,* of that simple vision to which truth offers itself like a landscape to the eye . . . [it is] beyond the sphere allotted to Man."[30]

Intellectus, unlike *ratio,* is not active work but is instead passive. It beholds and understands truth and beauty in the same way our eye perceives light or our ears sound. *Intellectus* finds its action in contemplation rather than observation. It can be described as the "aha" moment at the end of a geometric proposition, the moment when the full meaning of all the progressive steps seeps in and the light of understanding hits the geometer suddenly.

Because *intellectus* is "outside the sphere allotted to Man" and belongs to "the order of pure spirits," it is very hard to define and say exactly *what* it is; it is most commonly described through its characteristics and through what it looks like. *Intellectus* could be said to be more *the light of understanding*, where *ratio* is factual calculation. *Intellectus*, as more concerned with passivity and made possible through contemplation,

---

29. Pieper, *Leisure*, 28–29.
30. Pieper, *Leisure,* 28.

brings Man outside of himself; in its light, he abandons the sole pursuit of discursive logical reasonings with which he busies himself and waits upon the "muse" of understanding in a transcendental way.

These two forms of knowledge can be rather abstract in their descriptions, but they are an integral part of our encounter with the world. We utilize both *ratio* and experience *intellectus* constantly in our daily lives. To illustrate this, let us consider a real-life example.

Very early in my marriage, I was accustomed to preparing dinner for my wife and myself once a week. Not only did this practice give my wife a reprieve on date night, but it (supposedly) cultivated my own culinary capabilities. I was very happy with this weekly task (taking it on was my own idea), even though cooking, baking, and the like have never been a natural talent or strength of mine. Cooking has been an acquired, effort-driven skill for me. To this day, I am still not a very good chef.

Due to my inexperience and relative discomfort in meal prep, deciding *what* to make generally revolved around ingredients rather than grasping the overall concept of the finished dish. In other words, I chose meals based on a relatively short ingredient list and a simple recipe. One particular Thursday evening, I reached into my little recipe stash (filled with those little recipe tickets or coupons that grocery stores used to dispense as ideas for one product or another) and pulled out a relatively simple one using chicken, breadcrumbs, and oil. I think there was a vegetable included as well. In any event, this recipe fit the bill, and I assembled the required ingredients.

Thank goodness for that recipe, or else we would not have eaten that night. I prepared every step meticulously, following the letter of the formula with utmost diligence. I was completely lost without that slip of paper and constantly ran back and forth from the table to the counter to consult it for the next step or to clarify something on my current step. In any case, the whole exercise took me probably twice as long as it would have taken my wife, but I kept at it.

It was not until the chicken was covered in the pan that I had a dawning realization. The dish I made was a variation of fried chicken, plain and simple. There was absolutely nothing complex about it. In fact, had I realized what it was I was making, I probably could have intuited the recipe, or at least figured it out pretty close to how it actually should have been, my own bumbling kitchen experience notwithstanding. I laughed out loud at my own blindness, smirked with a little embarrassment, and chalked the incident up to more experience and a good story. I can honestly say that I have had *better* chicken than I had that night, but never one I have enjoyed procuring so much.

Hopefully, this illustration helps pin down the use of *ratio* and the experience of *intellectus*. *Ratio* was the driving factor and the operating principle for most of the episode. Gathering ingredients, preparing each individual one, and following the recipe step-by-step in order to reach a specific and particular conclusion is a very good example of the work that *ratio* cannot help but be. This, we would say, is the work or experience proper to Man and to this world. It is an operation that even a machine can be programmed to do. However, realizing as a subject an encounter with the whole, seeing everything fall into place in one instant by taking a step back and reflecting on what has been done, is the passive experience of *intellectus*. At that moment, I was *forced* to abandon what had been a blinding focus on the individual parts and behold the whole of the project as it was. I encountered a dish and saw it as a coherent object—not as so many isolated parts.

I could very well have completed the task, eaten my fill, and washed the dishes without ever having the realization of the whole. Eventually, I like to think my wife would have pointed it out sooner or later, but the fact remains: Without contemplation, I very well may have sat there at the table and eaten an abstract meal made up of ingredients and a formula. I say *may* have sat there because that is the thing about *intellectus*: It is passive and not guaranteed. In fact, I may have had the same disassociated experience of my meal in *spite* of taking that step back: The dawn of understanding is not the automatic result of a formula properly followed.

The operation of these two forms of knowledge working together is called *dialectic* (or, in Greek, *dianoia*), and was considered *the* proper way to think and encounter the world in classical philosophy.

Dialectic

In concluding his allegory of the cave, Plato and Glaucon come to the realization that "certain professors of education must be wrong when they say that they can put a knowledge into the soul which was not there before, like [putting] sight into blind eyes."[31] Rather, Plato posits that the power to learn is existent in every Man already. Education was seen as a journey toward understanding, a work-in-progress that lasts a whole lifetime. This journey made its primary tool *ratio*, observing and logically reasoning about the things of the world and the sciences of the day.

However, even though *ratio* was heavily employed and was the chief leader in the pursuit of understanding, it was not the end in itself. There came a certain point at which the mind had to be left to itself and would not be able to follow any further, even though the educator does "his best [to lead the student on, the student then] beholds not an image only but the absolute truth [itself]."[32] This point of departure from the discursive leadership of *ratio* to the sight of "the truth itself" is the moment of passive contemplation, wherein *intellectus* is made possible. The complete use of reason in this

31. Plato, *The Republic,* 270.
32. Plato, *The Republic,* 292.

way, utilizing and gaining both kinds of knowledge together, is called *dialectic*.

Dialectic is the complete operation of reason within the mind of Man to perceive the whole of creation. Reason is not a matter of one or the other—Man's knowledge is both *ratio* and *intellectus* simultaneously. It is a journey toward true knowledge in which the human mind allows itself to be led by *ratio* in pursuit of *intellectus* in one combined act of knowledge: the "discursive element fused with 'intellectual contemplation.'"[33] *Ratio* is human reason proper and is both prior to and necessary for understanding—it is true work. However, *ratio* leads the reason outside of itself and, through contemplation, encounters its fulfillment through *intellectus*, which is beyond the sphere of humans and exists as a true image of divine knowledge.

We are able to build an entire city (or fry a whole chicken) when we have memorized the propositions of geometry (or the recipe). Nonetheless, we remain within ourselves if we do not contemplate and *understand* those propositions in the light of *intellectus*. Seeing these two forms of knowledge together, we can say that *ratio* is the leading principle of human reason, utilizing the data perceived by the senses and categorizes, reasons, and discerns facts about this data. It only does so, however, in order to reach a more complete realization of the thing itself in *intellectus* knowledge.

---

33. Pieper, *Leisure*, 29.

As the crown and glory of understanding, *intellectus* gives *ratio* the means of fulfilling its end. *Intellectus* allows for a relationship between two forms of knowledge that are at once distinct *from* each other and yet share the same fundamental nature as oriented toward true knowledge. *Intellectus* is the knowledge most appropriate to *persons* in the Thomistic tradition. It "'is necessary for the perfection of human society,' . . . *nota bene,* necessary not only for the good of the individual who so devotes himself, but for the good of human society."[34] This necessary creation of *intellectus* is mirrored in Eve's creation as necessary not only for the perfection of Adam but for the completion of Man as a whole.

34. Pieper, *Leisure*, 41.

Modernity and Beyond: The Loss and Return of Reason

Classical philosophy assumes that we can obtain a sure knowledge of reality based on what we perceive through our senses. In the course of human experience, this premise at once presents something of a problem. The senses provide somewhat subjective data. People consistently observe or experience the same physical reality, only to find one was mistaken in their concluding judgments. Moreover, the senses vary *so* much from person to person that sometimes there is disagreement over what the senses *actually* perceive in the first place! Finally, in the fallen world, the senses sometimes fail the individual subject altogether, such as in cases of blindness, deafness, etc.

For classical philosophy, these problems were no obstacle: *of course,* the senses sometimes did not perceive the world accurately. But with the grace of God or through enough discussion and contemplation on common ground from a mutual understanding of what was already known about the world, such shortcomings could be overcome. It was taken as a matter of common sense that the world outside of Man's consciousness exists and can be perceived.

For a less secure thinker, however, the failing of the senses would present a chaotic chasm that could never be crossed with surety. During the Enlightenment period, alternative approaches to knowledge and thought began to emerge, arresting the insecurities of thinkers who only rested with the "sure knowledge" of mathematics, etc., and which could not trick the thinker with the subjectivity of the senses. This is the philosophy which has made its way to the modern day, ushering in a world of skeptic thinking[35] and relative morality. And the man we have to thank for this trajectory is, at least in part, René Descartes.

Many hold Descartes to be the father of modernity, and he was indeed an influential thinker of the Enlightenment period. It would not be *strictly* true to blame him single-handedly for introducing philosophical skepticism to the world; such musings were already

---

35. *Skeptic thinking,* or holding *everything* under scrutiny and starting from scratch for every individual person on every single conclusion, is called *skepticism.*

festering among academics of the day. Descartes was both an inheritor of those who came before and also of those contemporary to him, just as we ourselves are. Thus, while we cannot truthfully call Descartes the originator of modern absurdities, we can truthfully point to him as the crystallizing figure of the tensions which, prior to him, had no significant widespread meaningful or impactful form.

While classical philosophy is concerned with a more *intellectus*-based knowledge, the Enlightenment introduced a school of reasoning in search of only active knowledge—categorizable, logical, *ratio*-based knowledge. Facts in this school become nothing more than "collector's items, to be gathered in with the same kind of enthusiasm that at other times has informed the collection of Spode china or the numbers of railway engines."[36] This new school of thought forsakes any notion of a further telos beyond the individual thing itself; as an unintended consequence, it destroys the innate ability of Man to grasp knowledge as it is. Not only is it no longer the final end of Man's reason to recognize the cosmos in its fullness, but "reason [can] supply no genuine comprehension of Man's true end; that power of reason was destroyed by the fall of Man [capitalization mine]."[37]

Human reason in this light cannot comprehend essences. It is reduced to a calculative power:

---

36. MacIntyre, *After Virtue*, 79.
37. MacIntyre, *After Virtue*, 53.

> It can assess truths of fact and mathematical relations but nothing more. In the realm of practice, therefore, it can speak only of means. About ends it must be silent. Reason cannot even, as Descartes believed, refute skepticism; and hence a central achievement of reason according to Pascal, is to recognize that our beliefs are ultimately founded on nature, custom and habit.[38]

Understanding, passive reception, and contemplation of essences now had no place in metaphysics. No disposition is needed for "knowledge." All that is needed is a calculative mind, quick enough to solve equations. There is no end, no telos to modernity; it pursues knowledge of facts for its own sake.

Cartesian Skepticism

What is this philosophy from Descartes, the essential pioneer of the new epistemology? Descartes begins with the premise that it is within the nature of Man to be endowed with reason. However, he takes this to mean that the "diversity of our opinions does not arise from the fact that some people are more reasonable than others, but solely from the fact that we lead our thoughts along different paths and do not take the same things into consideration."[39] Descartes, arrested by the reality that the physical senses of Man can deceive the

---

38. MacIntyre, *After Virtue*, 54.
39. Descartes, *Discourse on Method*, 1.

individual through the subjective experience of the physical world, turns to mathematics as a model of knowledge whose reasonings were not reliant on the faulty senses but were universally "solid and firm."

Mathematics, for Descartes, encapsulates the peak of human reasoning capabilities. So long as the individual's reason was functioning properly and there was no interference by the senses, mathematical equations could, by nature, *not* be misleading—assuming the correct data was provided and the equations were executed using the right formula. He "was astonished by the fact that no one had built anything more noble upon [these] foundations"[40] and inquired whether there was anything in the world that would allow him the same level of certainty as mathematical equations could. He decided to "pretend that all things that had ever entered [his] mind were no more true than illusions of [his] dreams,"[41] and so began to construct a worldview based *not* on sensory presumptions. In his project, he determined to hold as true only those things that could be proven with *mathematical* certainty from his base of radical skepticism.

Out of this attempt at isolated thought, Descartes uttered his famous *Cogito, ergo sum*—a foundational recognition that if he was *thinking*, then he must first *exist.* Descartes held this realization as a fact "so firm and so assured that all the most extravagant suppositions of

40. Descartes, *Discourse on Method*, 5.
41. Descartes, *Discourse on Method*, 18.

the skeptics were incapable of shaking it, [and] judged that [he] could accept it without scruple as the first principle of the philosophy [he] was seeking."[42] From this, he concludes that he could "take as a general rule that the things we conceive very clearly and very distinctly are all true, but that there is merely some difficulty in properly discerning which are those that we distinctly conceive."[43]

Through a radical revolution of thought, rejecting all data the senses had to offer, Descartes stumbled across a principle many philosophers prior to him began with. That Man is conscious has, through history, been a testimony or proof that the thinker himself, as a subject, exists. However, with no foundation of Man as a unified body-soul composite, Descartes devolves all thinking from one of wonder and contemplation to a school of unwarranted skepticism. The search for truth was thus transformed into the pursuit of one particular *manner* of truth as if it were the fullness of understanding. This new epistemological method was unbecoming of both Man and the created order.

Descartes's method of epistemology and his discourse on reason mark a turning point in philosophy from a journey toward *intellectus* to the pursuit of *ratio* as an end by itself. Descartes's philosophy sought to forsake the pursuit of knowledge that was contemplative, not guaranteed to occur to the thinker, and based

42. Descartes, *Discourse on Method*, 18.
43. Descartes, *Discourse on Method*, 19.

on subjective, sensory-based conclusions (therefore also somewhat unpredictable). The new epistemology intends to trade classical knowledge for a philosophy only aimed at the concrete and categorizable, relishing the security offered by the latter.

Far from admitting any sort of value or reality to the subjective experience we gain from the senses, the new epistemology posits that we can't trust anything that the senses tell us because they are unverifiable by themselves. The world in this light embarked on a pursuit of truth whose first starting principle could only be that "all bodies, together with the space in which they are, must be considered nothing but mere representations in us, and exist nowhere but in our own thought."[44] Such a starting premise tragically isolates us within ourselves, removing human thought and experience from the outside world. Man, with this worldview, not only distrusts his own senses but also is forced to distrust the knowledge that anyone *else* might give him. If our own senses are unverifiable and untrustworthy, how much less must we trust others' senses!

---

44. Immanuel Kant, *Prolegomena to Any Future Metaphysics: And the Letter to Marcus Herz, February 1772*, trans. James W. Ellington (Indianapolis, IN: Hackett Publishing Company, 2010), "First Part Transcendental Question," remark II, 288, Kindle.

The Enduring Consequences of Cartesian Skepticism

The new epistemology arising after Descartes shifts knowledge from a study of how we know *things* to how we *give* things their meanings. Understanding ends consequentially becomes knowing only the purpose to which we put things. Modernity denies both telos and objective form; since we can only talk about what data is observed, or rather *appears* to be observed, the terms *telos* and *form* are replaced with *context* and *purpose*. Without ends, we can know not only nothing about the *nature* of the object itself, but nothing about the *moral weight* of the object. It now becomes possible to discuss a watch's nature *outside* of the framework of a "good watch."

In modernity, we can derive no objective morality or *ought*-based actions from the created order. In fact, we can really derive *no* concrete conclusions of the physical order whatsoever. At best, one can only assert that the "objects of our senses [existing] outside us are given, but we know nothing of what they may be in themselves, knowing only their appearances, i.e., the representations which they cause in us by affecting our senses."[45] As a result, we only reason about and understand things by the context in which we experience them or by what we want of them. The major innovation here is the assertion that things don't have

---

45. Kant, *Prolegomena to Any Future Metaphysics*, 289.

a nature, that *we* give things significance, either as individuals or as a community.

Modernity bases itself solely on mathematically sure premises. As such, it claims it is impossible to have in the conclusion anything which is not already present in the premise. In this school, all we can see is the data as it appears. Since we can't detect moral goodness as perceivable data, we can, therefore, make no moral judgment about a thing. In other words, "an argument in which any attempt is made to derive a moral or evaluative conclusion from factual premises, something which is not in the premises, namely the moral or evaluative element, will appear in the conclusion."[46] It would be as if the moral conclusion of the object were pulled out of thin air, with no perceivable relation to the object at hand.

This practical impossibility of making "ought" conclusions from "is" premises "becomes an inescapable truth for philosophers whose culture possesses only the impoverished moral vocabulary which results."[47] In this, we see the basis for a demand for complete autonomous freedom in the world today. Each individual is "prior to and apart from all roles." He perceives the world for himself and cannot ever be sure whether the world he has perceived is accurate or even *exists* in its own right. Each individual must, therefore, be

46. MacIntyre, *After Virtue,* 57.
47. MacIntyre, *After Virtue*, 59.

left alone to do the best he can in a world only he can perceive.

A Return to Reason

The philosophical problems modernity causes are not *normal* problems. Becoming arrested in the face of human subjectivity, concluding that since we cannot obtain *rati-ic* knowledge about the whole of creation, we must then not be able to conclude *anything* objectively, raises questions that are absurd—but coherent enough to render them difficult to refute. Reason is changed from aiming toward a contemplative, receptive movement within the soul in response to the reality encountered. It no longer intuits or concludes the purpose, nature, and moral relevance of the object in question. Reason is instead an isolated mind prison, trapped and reduced to nothing more than raw data collection. Such a transformation necessarily results in each individual imposing meaning onto objects, dictating and ruling reality for themselves.

One might be forgiven for attempting an absolute return to Aquinas and classical philosophy as a solution to these problems. Solely turning back to Aquinas is historicism, however, both unnecessary and impossible. Phenomenology, introduced by Husserl, gives us a way to go beyond the split. It introduces a school that allows the individual to get to perennial philosophy, exploring the theory of realism without the failings of modernity.

As a new and developing philosophical discipline, phenomenology has much to offer the world. Alas, we do not have adequate time to fully discuss it here. We must confine ourselves to pointing out only those key points, allowing us to reconcile modernity's subjectivist objections and Thomistic epistemology. However, for anyone who wishes to take a deep dive into the good things phenomenology has to offer, Robert Sokolovski's *Introduction to Phenomenology* is an invaluable resource. Looking deeper into this discipline allows for a path forward from Cartesian modernity, acknowledging its legitimate problems while avoiding its absurdities. In our discussion here, however, we are concerned overall not so much with phenomenology *as such*, but rather Karol Wojtyła's use of its principles as applied to Thomistic personalism. As a result, we only mention phenomenology in its own right briefly and in passing.

Wojtyła utilizes several of Husserl's assertions in his reconciling modernity with Aquinas. Husserl states that the world is public, not private. In his view, mistakes are not made in the recesses of the mind but within the boundaries of the public world. The mind remains intent on the object of its perception, encountering the appearance of the object and abstracting knowledge from the appearance itself. Phenomenology presupposes there is an actual object to encounter, not simply a projection of the individual.

It is this world that Wojtyła enters into and restores the Thomistic concept of personhood and man's ability to know the world, even in an *intellect-ic* way. He accomplishes this by asserting that the *subjective experience* of the individual is a part of the person, which is of particular importance—not merely a variable within the epistemological process that renders knowledge subjective and relative.

Absurd as modernity's conclusions might be, its subjective premise of individual sensory experience bears some merit and must be accounted for. Wojtyła holds that what is legitimate can be reconciled with Thomistic epistemology. According to Wojtyła, Aquinas uses the Boethian definition of a *person* as "*rationalis naturae individua substantia,*"[48] or an individual substance of a rational nature. Valuable as this definition is, it does not account for the unique perception of reality seen through the eyes of each individual human being. "Human thought," Wojtyła writes, "has a creative character; it is the basis of creativity and the source of culture . . . We are by nature creators, not just consumers. We are creators because we think. And because our thought is also the basis of our personalities, one could say that we are creators because we are

48. Karol Wojtyła, *Person and Community: Selected Essays,* Catholic Thought from Lublin, trans. Theresa H. Sandok (New York, NY: Lang, 2008), 167.

persons."[49] It is not enough to declare that objective reality exists, exploring the ways in which we perceive that objective reality, for we are not mere consumers of sensory perception. The particular subject's experience of that reality is a *real* experience in itself, born of individual interpretation and subjective sensory faculties.

Theologically, this makes sense. If we are to accept that all of reality is the *vestigia* of God through which He makes Himself present to His children, then the particular ways He presents Himself to the mind of the subject through the senses must count for something. This is one way that we can understand completely different conclusions and experiences from the same event. This is also how we can account for the apparent deception we can find within the senses so foundational to the problems suffered by Descartes.

---

49. Wojtyła, *Person and Community*, 179.

Anamnesis: Knowledge of the Moral Order, the Natural Law

Thus far, our discussion has revolved around the relationship between *ratio* and *intellectus,* and how the relative philosophies throughout history have valued one or the other in either a complete approach or exclusive rejection of epistemology. These two forms of knowledge make up the faculty of human reason, of rational thought properly speaking. However, there remains one more form of knowledge that we must consider: the knowledge all Men have of the *natural law,* the moral order written on the hearts of Man.

Most discussions on epistemology would not include any treatment of the *conscience*, of how we *know* right from wrong. As such, we might be forgiven if, at first, we do not make a clear connection between our discussion thus far and the introduction of the conscience as a form of knowledge. And yet, the concept of the conscience is so integral to our further discussions and *is* in itself a form of knowledge that it would be a fatal mistake for us to omit a reflection on it here.

Somewhere deep within the consciousness of Man, there is a fire sparked—a spark of love, which has been put into us by the Creator, meaning: "We have received interiorly beforehand the capacity and disposition for observing all divine commandments."[50] This disposition toward the good operates in such a way that the knowledge of basic right and wrong is, in a sense, "recognized" by each individual within himself. The soul of Man, in one sense, sees "all things that exist, whether in this world or in the world below; and it is not wonder that she should be able to call to remembrance all that she ever knew about virtue . . . for all enquiry and all learning is but recollection."[51]

In a certain way, knowledge of the moral order through the natural law is thereby not unlike what we described as *intellectus*: *Anamnesis* is indeed related to the *intellectus* form of knowledge inasmuch as it is passive. *Anamnesis* rises from within the consciousness of Man, as if already existing there.

---

50. Joseph Ratzinger, "Systematic Consequences: The Two Levels of Conscience," in *On Conscience: Two Essays* (San Francisco, CA: Ignatius Press, 2007), chapter 1, Kindle.
51. Plato, *Meno,* 443.

Recollection in Platonic Dialogues

The concept of knowledge as *recollection* is central to the Platonic dialogues, perhaps most memorably in his notion of memory from the *Meno.* In this short work, Socrates is inquiring as to what virtue might be and stumbles upon some trouble defining it through discussion with his friend, Meno. He asserts that they could "recollect" the definition of *virtue,* that the soul had been reincarnated again and again and had already encountered everything. As a result, knowledge already exists within the soul of the person.

Socrates supposedly demonstrates the soul's inherent ability to recognize the truth as if already present within itself by drawing out of an unlearned slave boy a geometric proposition about the area of a square. Almost in the style of a magician, Socrates essentially asks Meno to choose a volunteer from the audience: "You call one of your numerous attendants, that I may demonstrate on him."[52] Once a suitable boy has been identified (unlearned in geometry and speaks Greek), Socrates draws an image of a square. He begins to ask the boy a series of questions about the shape and area of the square.

The boy follows Socrates's line of questioning, but the conclusion the boy draws ends up being incorrect. Though he becomes initially convinced that the area of the 2'x 2' square is eight feet (the sum of all the

52. Plato, *Meno*, 444.

sides), the boy comes to recognize that this is, in fact, incorrect. Guided by further questions from Socrates, the boy moves from being convinced of his erroneous opinion to the realization that not only was his opinion wrong, but also that he did not know the truth of a square's area at all. Finally, by answering the questions posed to him, the boy eventually comes to realize and affirm the correct area of the square.

The key feature of this exercise was that Socrates merely asked the boy questions. At no point did he *feed* answers to the child. Though the child followed Socrates's lead and gave his assent or denial to his questions, the child was never handed or instructed on the truth:

All these answers [were] given out of his own head."[53] Thus, Socrates concludes that knowledge is not really something *learned* as in imposed, filled, or instilled from an outside source. To *learn* is therefore really to have knowledge "just been stirred up in him, as in a dream . . . Without anyone teaching him he will recover his knowledge for himself, if he is only asked questions.[54]

This exercise leads Socrates (Plato) to conclude that "the truth of all things always existed in the soul" because "the soul is immortal."[55] Plato has Socrates then explain how the soul could possibly *know* the truth as

53. Plato, *Meno,* 450.
54. Plato, *Meno,* 450.
55. Plato, *Meno,* 451.

always having existed there by simply recounting one of his famous reincarnation myths.

It is worth it to take a brief sidetrack in our discussion to point out that the jury is still out as to whether Plato himself ever believed any of these myths; I would wager that he did not. For being such a smart man and having the right judgment on so much, it seems a bit odd that he would believe so many myths. I say this for two reasons.

For one, the myths he tells are not the same ones across the dialogues—even if he is trying to illustrate the same point. As a result, he usually cautions his listener with either a similar phrase to "Mark, now, and see whether their words are true,"[56] or even, "Whether what I told you would or would not have been a reality I cannot venture to say; but you would have seen something like reality."[57] Furthermore, the deeper point he was making using these myths is actually true. The soul *does* have intuitive and solid knowledge of things, especially as it pertains to the moral order in

---

56. Plato, *Meno,* 443.
57. Plato, *The Republic,* 292.

the natural law.[58] This knowledge does not come from reincarnation, however. The soul has knowledge of inherent goodness because of an imprint in the hearts of Men by God at Man's creation. Man accesses this knowledge in a way much like true memory, a recognition of the good when encountered, or a recollecting.

---

58. To continue for a bit more on our sidetrack, even the early Church Fathers utilized Platonic imagery when describing the afterlife, especially concerning the souls of the damned: "Plato said that Rhadamanthus and Minos would punish the wicked who came before them; and we say that this is what will happen, but at the hand of Christ, and to the same bodies, reunited with their souls and destined for eternal punishment, and not for a thousand-year period only, as he said" (Justin Martyr, *First Apology,* in *The First and Second Apologies*, trans. L. W. Barnard (New York, NY: Paulist Press, 1997), paragraph 8, 27.
Later on, Justin Martyr writes concerning the relative commonality of divine reality within philosophical thinkers of gentile origin: "There seem to be seeds of truth among all people, but they are proved not to have understood them accurately when they contradict each other" ("First Apology," paragraph 44, 53–54). In this, I think we can at least entertain the idea that for someone as smart as Plato, mythological imagery was used because it was what was at hand, was understandable at the time, and was sort of the best one could do without the gift of direct divine revelation. The fact that he would hit upon some very real beliefs of the early Christians without divine revelation bears witness to the fact that through our reason we are able to come to certain knowledge of some deeper truths of the world, and even if we may be lacking in ability to understand *how* it might be possible, we can come to knowledge *that* it is possible.

This *"remembering,"* in Christian thought, is called *anamnesis*.

Anamnesis, though distinct and not the same, can be colloquially equated with the Christian idea of *conscience,* the "most secret core and sanctuary of a man, where he is alone with God, whose voice echoes in his depths."[59] [60] Here, in the core of his consciousness, the person cannot divorce himself from the basic principles of doing good and avoiding evil for no other reason than it seems good to act thus. Moreover, it is not a basic individual orientation toward *personal* goodness or values: on the contrary:

> In the depths of his conscience, man detects a law which he does not impose upon himself, but which holds him to obedience . . . There is profoundly imprinted upon it *a principle* vis-à-vis the *objective norm* which establishes and conditions the correspondence of its decisions with the commands and

---

59. John Paul II, *Dominum et Vivificantem*, para. 43.

60. It is very important that we do not make synonyms out of the terms *conscience* and *anamnesis.* The two are quite different in their scope and operation. However, their *general* end—"humans know to do good and avoid evil"—is similar. And so, at this time, while we are trying to focus on *anamnesis* specifically, it is not an unrelated topic to also discuss *conscience*.

No further clarification or distinction is warranted at this particular time. We will talk more about their distinction briefly in a later chapter.

> prohibitions which are at the basis of human behavior.[61]

How can we speak of this knowledge in any other way than a *recognition* of what is true, and toward that which brings us closer to God? And in this Plato is not far from the truth of the matter. How can we *recognize* something that is entirely foreign to our minds and that we have never encountered before? We could not, not unless "a basic understanding of the good had already been instilled in us."[62]

We each have, in fact, encountered the moral order before: not in a prior life through reincarnation (which, again, I doubt even Plato believed to be the case); rather, we have encountered it at the very moment of our creation. We behold it once more through a recognition of what already exists within the mind of God, *even if we do not attest to the existence of God Himself.* "The conscience is the voice of God, even when man recognizes in it nothing more than the principle of the moral order which it is not humanly possible to doubt, even without any direct reference to the Creator."[63] The inner orientation toward God "involves all people, even those who do not know Christ and his Gospel or God himself."[64]

---

61. John Paul II, *Dominum et Vivificantem*, para. 43.
62. Ratzinger, *On Conscience*, 31.
63. John Paul II, *Dominum et Vivificantem*, para. 43.
64. John Paul II, *Veritatis Splendor* (Vatican City: Vatican Press, 1993), paragraph 3.

Recollection in Christian Thought

In classical epistemology, *moral order* is an intrinsic characteristic of the perceivable world. Our example of a watch as inseparable from the concept of a "good" watch demonstrates the intelligible morality we can perceive simply from encountering an object and contemplating its form. This moral order exists because it has already been thought in the mind of God and is constantly present to His own mind. In truth, *everything* exists within the mind of God, including objects and the moral order into which those objects fall. Through rational thought, we experience a "remembering," not because the thinker already knows it or came to it on his own as if it were a "store of retrievable contents,"[65] but because it exists outside of Man and within God. In this, *all* forms of knowledge can, in one sense, be related to the workings of *anamnesis*. It is not so much that all knowledge can be accessed within the recesses of Man's heart like the moral order can, but rather, Man can *recognize* truth (to a more or less accurate extent and inasmuch as God is truth) when he encounters it. He brings himself up into this divine knowledge and participates in the ever-present and already-thought mind of God.

Just as *anamnesis* lends itself well to a previous point about knowledge of reality through an object's telos and ends, it offers an important insight into

---

65. Ratzinger, *On Conscience*, 31

the truth of Man's nature and purpose, specifically. Whether Plato believed the myths within his dialogues or not, the point he was trying to make stands: "If the truth of all things always existed in the soul, then the soul is immortal."[66] It is precisely because of his ability to *know and see* the inherent goodness of the moral order that we can know the immortality of the soul and "that a man ought to live always in perfect holiness."[67]

Anamnesis as evidence for the soul's immortality is not restricted to Plato. Christian thinkers agree with him. In his book *On Conscience*, Ratzinger echoes the fact that it is through *anamnesis* that we can know the immortality of the soul. Because the immortality of the soul can never be isolated from the immortality of God, *anamnesis* provides the image of Man as immortal only insofar as he is created in the image of God—not by virtue of the knowledge of things within his soul. This is why we can still speak of individuals who do *not* attest to the existence of God both as being themselves *immortal*, created *in the image of God* and have themselves the purpose and, therefore, *obligation* of pursuing God:

> [T]he first so-called ontological level of the phenomenon conscience consists in the fact that something like an original memory of the good and true (they are identical) has been implanted in us, that there is an inner ontological

66. Plato, *Meno,* 451.
67. Plato, *Meno,* 443.

> tendency within man, who is created in the likeness of God, toward the divine. From its origin, man's being resonates with some things and clashes with others. This anamnesis of the origin, which results from the god-like constitution of our being, is not a conceptually articulated knowing, a store of retrievable contents. It is, so to speak, an inner sense, a capacity to recall, so that the one whom it addresses, if he is not turned in on himself, hears its echo from within. He sees: That's it! That is what my nature points to and seeks.[68]

This very ability to "remember" the truth about the moral order and natural law, the "capacity to command what is good and to forbid evil, placed in Man by the Creator, *is the main characteristic of the personal subject.*"[69] The recognition offered by *anamnesis* allows Man to exist within the world of the whole of reality. It allows him access to divine truths which are beheld by the mind of God and which do not need Man's own personal experience, limited as it is by the potential of faulty senses and subject to individual incorrect reasoning.

Brief Clarification on Terms

We cannot go much farther without clarifying some terms we have been and will be using. There are,

---

68. Ratzinger, *On Conscience*, 31–32.
69. John Paul II, *Dominum et Vivificantem*, para. 43.

generally speaking, three terms denoting innate knowledge of good versus evil, and which outline our understanding of the natural moral order written on the hearts of Men. These terms are *conscience, anamnesis*, and *synderesis*. Those of you reading who are more philosophically inclined may have already noted the absence of two of these terms, and questioned why there seems to be an almost unwarranted overlap between *anamnesis* and *conscience* in this section.

While our intention is definitely *not* to write a philosophy textbook bogged down with technical differences, clarity of language is important in our conversations. And so, while neither conscience nor *synderesis* feature prominently in the rest of this book, I find it somewhat necessary to clarify and make the necessary distinction between these three terms, so that I am not mistaken for saying something I am actually *not* in fact saying.

The clarifications and distinctions that follow are far from comprehensive and are intended more for discursive clarity rather than exhaustive precision. To that end, if the distinctions offered are less than complete and precise, I hope that you will forgive me in favor of moving forward toward our end.

The *conscience* is, according to Aquinas, not so much an activity or property of the intellect as much as it is an operation of the will. Its object is, according to him, the Good understood. We will discuss this distinction a tad bit more in the following chapters, but essentially, it drives the person to *know* and *understand* the Good by choosing and *acting* upon the Good.

Anamnesis, while clearly related to the *conscience*, is not precisely the same. For our purposes, we have placed it within the realm of the intellect, *not* the will. It is not so much a driving force causing us to choose one thing or another as much as it is *recognizing* the Good when we encounter it. This is a deeply personal operation, as the word *encounter* cannot help but intimate.

Anamnesis is not necessarily or even primarily a recognition of the Good as in "it is good that I do not murder people" as much as it is a recognition of the Good when we live it, when we choose it in our daily lives—when we *encounter* it. We cannot encounter *not murdering* someone; we *can* encounter the Good in loving our neighbor, living according to our vocation, etc. We will discuss this *encountering* and its personal properties in depth in the following chapters.

Synderesis is the final of the three terms we need to clarify. It is, in short, the acknowledgement of the natural moral order. We could talk about it in terms of "first principles," such as it is wrong to murder someone, generally speaking, do good and avoid evil, etc. Synderesis does not concern itself with the Good understood or recognizing the Good itself; it rather causes us to acknowledge that there is "a" good, generally.

Here is how the three together might play out in a specific but very limited scenario. Synderesis causes me to know that it is not only bad for me to kill my father, but that it is good for me to honor him (general principle). The conscience causes me to understand this good by actively honoring him as my parent: obey him, give him a card for Father's Day, engrave a humorous motto on a new knife, etc. (specific application to adhere to the first principles). Finally, *anamnesis* causes me to recognize/resonate, etc. Goodness itself in the deeply personal elements of my honoring my father—and to find fulfillment of my personal vocation when I act thus. In fact, one might suppose that I only chose *those particular* actions to honor my father *because those particular actions are the way I am predisposed to bond with him*. Thus, whereas the conscience would have me seek to honor him further, *anamnesis* would cause me to honor him according to my personality, which is precaused by the way in which I recognize what is legitimately good.

If this brief sidetrack has seemed extraneous to some and grossly oversimplified to others, I humbly ask your pardon. This distinction between these three operations is simply beyond what I hope to cover in these pages. And yet, the nature of the words we are using seems to dictate that we take a few minutes to clarify.

Synderesis and conscience will not play a prominent part in the rest of this book. In fact, synderesis will not feature at all beyond this point, while we will only treat conscience sparingly. However, we will discuss the practical applications of *anamnesis* in much further detail in the following chapters.

Conclusion

What shall we conclude, then, about the nature of *anamnesis* as a form of knowledge? *Anamnesis* is a different form of knowledge altogether from either *ratio* or *intellectus.* We can use *ratio* to come to certain knowledge about what the moral order is and, likewise, *how* we know about it. Similarly, we can behold the fullness of the moral order in contemplation and wonder at the magnificence of the created world. In this, *ratio* and *intellectus* are related to *anamnesis,* inasmuch as they are both movements within the soul. However, these two are functions of the intellect proper. In truth, *anamnesis* is not an *action* of the intellect at all but is more akin to an orientation. It is a recognition of something already beheld by *the* Person from all time in the divine mind of God. Man recognizes this because he is created *in* the image of God.

Concluding Knowledge

Man desires to understand. Though this desire is evidenced by his rational faculties, Man's capacity for reason is not the *origin* of that desire. Man's desire for true knowledge is a consequence of his most basic orientation, manifesting in a desire to act according to what is *actually* true and what is *really* good—not what is deemed good according to personal preferences or desires. Man is not content to look toward the good he already harbors within his heart without pursuing the technical *why* of the good: what *makes* it good and in what *way* is it true. As a result, Man can and does categorize the reality he encounters around him, marking every appearance and sensation received from the senses in their own particular manner as accounting for something. His intellect is capable of many things, even encountering the whole of reality and the communicated therein by beholding reality according to its own right: a comprehensive whole operating on a level that goes beyond that which can be observed and charted.

It is true that Man must utilize his senses to perceive the categorical and perceivable realities of the physical world through the function of *ratio.* However, the categorizing of perceived data is not the fullness of knowledge his intellect longs for. It is only when he can rise above the simple observations rooted in reality and behold the fullness of the observed thing that Man fully utilizes his intellect and can see things as they are.

Chapter II

Human Person: Body and Soul

"Why wouldn't you like to see a human body with a curling tail with a crest of ostrich feathers at the end? Because it would be useless and pointless. Because the beauty of the human body is that it hasn't a single muscle which doesn't serve its purpose; that there's not a line wasted; that every detail of it fits one idea, the idea of a man and the life of a man."
Ayn Rand, (*The Fountainhead, 1943*)

Philosophers through the ages have consistently recognized the spiritual attributes of Man—he is more than just his physical makeup. Man possesses an inner life, a spiritual element beyond the physical realm; this spiritual element is called his *soul.* The soul has passions that move the person with emotions and desires and is equipped with a will driving him to action. The will determines its action by virtue of what his intellect perceives as good and what he desires as bringing happiness.

As the previous chapter illustrated, Man has the innate desire to know. Man's nature as being endowed with intellect for rational thought has frequently been used to prove the immortality of his soul. Through his faculty of reason, he can understand certain things about the created order. Of himself, Man understands that he is, in a sense, *intended* for the pursuit of knowledge. All this is fine, but what is it that makes Man a *person,* with value? How do we *know* that we are intended for and must pursue an *intellect-ic* knowledge of the world—that we are, therefore, not merely special or high-functioning calculators? Welcome to Chapter II, where we will answer these questions.

We dealt briefly with *anamnesis* in the preceding chapter, seeing it as the defining point of the person as subject and actor. In this chapter, we shall explore *anamnesis* more fully as a movement at the core of our being. It is a movement which, coupled with the powers of the soul, allows us to have a clear image of the mystery that it is to be a person: an individual, unique and unrepeatable being, with a subjective experience of the created order, desiring to communicate his own unrepeatability with other persons in a community.

We shall discuss the responsibility each individual has toward another person when they live in a community, examining the claim that human dignity comes not from consciousness *per se,* but from the divine image of God imprinted on Man's heart. Upholding this dignity is the crucial point of existence, demanding that individuals avoid any sort of use or mere utility of the person. Karol Wojtyła calls this basic level of responsibility the *"personalistic norm,"* and the principles of this norm are the foundation of objective morality.

The Tripartite Soul of Plato

Man is not a creature of abstract thought alone. He enjoys a nature that causes him to use his body in knowing, desiring, and acting, coinciding with the idea that Man is a creative actor within the world. These three parts of the soul—the *intellect, passions,* and the *will*—are referred to together as constituting the *tripartite soul*.

Plato outlined the tripartite soul in his dialogue *The Republic.* In this dialogue, he constructs a hypothetical city so as to examine certain aspects of virtue and movements within the intellect. Through this thought experiment, Plato asserts that "the same principles which exist in the [the hypothetical] State exist also in the individual, and that they are three in number."[70]

---

70. Plato, *The Republic,* 166.

Man's rational nature demonstrates a natural hierarchy between these parts of the soul, "[with] one ruling principle of reason, and the two subject ones of spirit and desire are equally agreed that reason ought to rule, and [ought] not rebel."[71]

Plato's illustration of the parts of the soul and their relative hierarchy, with the passions and will necessarily subject to the intellect, is echoed in the *Phaedrus*. In this dialogue, the soul is likened to a charioteer, driving two-winged horses. He describes it this way:

> Now the winged horses and the charioteers of the gods are all of them noble and of noble descent, but those of other races are mixed; the human charioteer drives his in a pair; and one of them is noble and of noble breed, and the other is ignoble and of ignoble breed; and the driving of them of necessity gives a great deal of trouble to him.[72]

Plato does not stop at mere acknowledgment that the soul has the higher ability of reason that must rule over the lower parts. He goes on to assert that, because of its rational nature, we can know the soul itself is immortal. The soul is harnessed to a physical body, however, so that only in relation to the body can we

---

71. Plato, *The Republic,* 168.
72. Plato, *Phaedrus,* in *The Essential Plato*, trans. Benjamin Jowett and M. J. Knight (New York, NY: Quality Paperback Book Club, 1999), 805–806.

speak of the soul as being mortal. Switching to another dialogue, we find Plato explaining it this way:

> I will endeavor to explain to you in what way the mortal differs from the immortal creature. The soul or animate being has the care of the inanimate, and traverses the whole heaven in divers forms appearing;—when perfect and fully winged she soars upward, and is the ruler of the universe; while the imperfect soul loses her feathers, and drooping in her flight at last settles on the solid ground—there, finding a home, she receives an earthly frame which appears to be self-moved, but is really moved by her power; and this composition of soul and body is called a living and mortal creature. For no such union can be reasonably believed, or at all proved to be other than mortal; although fancy may imagine a god whom, not having seen nor surely known, we invent—such a one, an immortal creature having a body, and having also a soul which have been united in all time. Let that, however, be as God wills, and be spoken of acceptably to him. But the reason why the soul loses her feathers should be explained, and is as follows: The wing is intended to soar aloft and carry that which gravitates downwards into the upper region, which is the dwelling of the gods; and this is that element of the body which is most akin to the divine. Now the divine is beauty, wisdom, goodness, and the like; and by these the wing of the soul is nourished, and

> grows apace; but when fed upon evil and foulness, and the like, wastes and falls away.[73]

Sifting through the imagery of myth and getting to the truth of what Plato is speaking of, we can note several key points here:

1. That the immortal nature of the soul is due to its *spiritual nature* (this would be the higher functions, the intellect),
2. That we call it *living* when it is compounded with a physical body (for Plato, the body would be nothing more than a meat suit for the soul, but Aquinas would proceed with a more holistic view of the person),
3. And finally, it is only by virtue of being created in the likeness of a great being whose very nature is pure spirit and therefore cannot be corrupted that we can imagine a soul would be immortal.

Whether or not Plato believed the myths he puts forth as illustrations of more foundational principles is

73. Plato, *Phaedrus,* 806.

irrelevant here.[74] The conclusions he draws are valid and just as foundational for our own reasonings of today.

It is important to note that for Plato, the body is simply a vessel for the soul; it is subject to corruption and, therefore, must be denied and transcended if we are to ever live with a free spirit. For our purposes at this point, we must highlight the third point Plato illustrates. He holds that the soul is immortal inasmuch as it continues to be nourished by "beauty, wisdom, goodness, and all such qualities."

---

74. I tend to think more and more that Plato used mythological imagery as a tool that was available but did not, in fact, ascribe to the myths in his dialogues. What is more, early Christian writings can sometimes give us a glimpse as to how the Gentiles (such as Plato) would have reacted to hearing the words of some of the prophets of the Old Testament. On speaking of the freedom of the will, Justin Martyr quotes Plato but asserts that Plato was quoting Moses: "And so when Plato said, 'The blame is his who chooses, and God is blameless,' he took this from the prophet Moses and uttered it. For Moses is more ancient than all the Greek writers. And everything that both philosophers and poets have said concerning the immortality of the soul, or punishments after death, or contemplation of heavenly things, or doctrines like these, they have received such hints from the prophets as have enabled them to understand and expound these things" (Justin Martyr, *First Apology,* paragraph 44, 53).

Thomistic Personalism: Aquinas and Wojtyla

Aquinas

It might seem like a very large historical jump to begin with Plato (423 BC) and skip right to Thomas Aquinas's (AD 1225) dealings on the soul. In truth, it is not as much of a jump as it would seem. Aquinas utilizes Aristotelian lenses in his writings, accepting much of Aristotle's philosophy and science as outright accurate. Aquinas's examination of the soul is no exception. By examining Aquinas's treating of the soul, we also by default examine many aspects of the Aristotelian soul – Aristotle who was, as we have seen, largely the successor to Plato. Thus, Aquinas successfully bridges the philosophical gap between pagan Greece and Christian progress, offering a concise (if academic) description of how the soul operates. His work in this field is a vital component of understanding personhood from the philosophical perspective we are taking in this project. Alas, as we must do with so many of the historical giants thus far, we will only be able to briefly explore this topic as we continue on.

Aquinas's description of the powers of the soul is a technical and somewhat complex topic. Even though we encounter these powers and their operations on a daily basis, we experience them as a coherent whole—they are barely discernible in real time. Individually, their descriptions are such that it behooves us to start with a practical example in mind. To this end, let us consider the encounter a fellow soldier of mine had with a rattlesnake.

***

On my last deployment, I found myself working the night shift on a twenty-four-hour operation. Now, there were several aspects of the night shift—such as lack of sleep—that were less than desirable. However, there was one benefit that we *night walkers* (as we called ourselves) enjoyed exclusively: beating the heat. During the day, the temperatures would often rise to 112 degrees.

The high temperature, coupled with the lack of shade and direct sunlight, made it nearly impossible to engage in outside activities during daylight hours. The darkness provided a shade that dropped temperatures to a balmy 95 degrees and allowed us an opportunity to experience the outside as no other shift could.

Apparently, this arrangement also naturally appeals to certain cold-blooded (reptilian) desert predators. One particular night, my fellow soldier and I were about halfway through our shift when she decided to exit the building and make the short walk to our vehicle. The soldier had been outside barely three seconds when she burst back into the room, proclaiming, "Sergeant, there's a rattlesnake right outside!" And sure enough, even through the walls of the building serving as our tactical operations center (TOC), I could hear the unmistakable drone of a danger-noodle's rattle.

I popped my head outside to ascertain the initial whereabouts of the animal and to track its further movements. There, well within striking distance, was a little two-and-a-half-foot rattlesnake, raised up in a defensive position.

I considered taking care of it the old-fashioned way (I did fancy a new snakeskin band for my hat), but thought better of it. Instead, the soldier and I took the opportunity to discuss rattlesnake bite first aid, the environmental impact of snakes, and why the snake was out hunting at night when they are cold-blooded to begin with (it would seem better for a cold-blooded animal to capitalize on the intense sunlight).

After the initial assessment, we both went back inside. The snake, however, could still hear our voices through the thin walls of the TOC as he remained pressed up against the structure and continued rattling for almost two hours. After an extended period, he cautiously continued on his way. The snake settled in a relatively nearby position, remaining well camouflaged in the sparse but dried vegetation, and thus posed a potential risk to the oncoming shift. A removal was called in, and by the time the handler arrived, the snake had ceased to be surprised by us altogether. He did not even panic when he was picked up and transported elsewhere.

***

In this incident, we can see two sensory animals (soldier and snake) experiencing what amounts to basically the same event. In some ways, they react similarly toward each other. Their overall experiences, however, are characterized differently. Whereas the soldier describes her experience as one who was *surrounded* by the sound of the rattle and therefore endured an immediate, guttural reaction toward an unseen but clearly proximate danger, the snake (could he talk) would have described a different (but still startled) reaction altogether. Though both the snake and the soldier have *some* shared operations as living beings, their highest and driving powers are different. We will examine their experiences of the event through a Thomistic lens.

Aquinas accepts and builds on Plato's work on the soul in that he agrees that the soul has three parts: *intellect, will,* and *passions.* Not to be confused with these *parts* identified by Plato, Aquinas identifies five *powers* that exist within the tripartite soul. He relies on Aristotle's definitions of these powers according to *De Anima,* stating, "The Philosopher says (*De Anima* ii, 3), 'The powers are the vegetative, the sensitive, the appetitive, the locomotive, and the intellectual.'"[75] These powers all work together to offer the living being an experience of the world and are categorized into different operations. Though there are some shared powers among *all* living souls, only those powers operating in the souls of higher animals are pertinent to our larger discussion. We will only treat with the lower powers briefly.

Aquinas's distinction between the parts versus the powers of the soul is partly made as an explanation for seeing plants as living things. There *must* be recognition that every living thing has some animating principle (a soul). This "animating principle" is the specific difference between Aquinas and Plato on the soul's relation to the body. Plato is convinced that the soul is *encased* in the body. Aquinas, however, sees the soul as *an essential aspect of* the body that brings it to life and moves it according to its nature. Therefore, plants,

75. Thomas Aquinas, *Summa Theologiae*, q. 78, art. 1.

animals, and humans are all endowed with a soul—not simply with a physical medium wherein there exists a soul.

To speak of a plant having a soul is not to suppose it shares a higher function, such as is present in Man. Not all souls have all five powers. Higher animals have higher powers, whereas lower animals (and plants) only have those powers necessary for the soul to animate the object. Aquinas describes the hierarchy of these powers in this way:

> There exists an operation of the soul which so far exceeds the corporeal nature that it is not even performed by any corporeal organ; and such is the operation of the 'rational soul.' Below this, there is another operation of the soul, which is indeed performed through a corporeal organ, but not through a corporeal quality, and this is the operation of the 'sensitive soul;' for though hot and cold, wet and dry, and other such corporeal qualities are required for the work of the senses, yet they are not required in such a way that the operation of the senses takes place by virtue of such qualities; but only for the proper disposition of the organ. The lowest of the operations of the soul is that which is performed by a corporeal organ, and by virtue of a corporeal quality. Yet this transcends the operation of the corporeal nature; because the movements of bodies are caused by an extrinsic principle, while these operations are from an intrinsic

> principle; for this is common to all the operations of the soul; since every animate thing, in some way, moves itself. Such is the operation of the "vegetative soul" for digestion, and what follows, is caused instrumentally by the action of heat.[76]

From this passage, we can identify conceptually how we might speak of a plant as being alive. Plants are alive because they have a *soul* (that is, an animating principle). However, different souls have different powers according to their nature, as Aquinas distinguishes. The most basic powers, necessarily shared among all living things, are the vegetative (and possibly the locomotive). So, a plant's soul, for example, would look something like this: A plant is most naturally in a *vegetative state* (it is constantly at "rest," wherein it takes nutrition, it grows, and it reproduces), and thus plants exhibit *vegetative power*.

All souls (forms of life) have a vegetative power and the power (in one limited capacity or another) of locomotion: "Every animate thing, in some way, moves itself." In our example at the beginning of this section, we can see that the rattlesnake grows, takes in nutrition, reproduces, and moves. So, too, does my fellow soldier have all these powers. However, whereas a plant's capabilities usually cease here, both the snake and the soldier can move more or less freely, engage

---

76. Aquinas, *Summa Theologiae,* q. 78, art. 1.

with the world with emotive responses, and have some limited cognition, desire, and experience of the world. And the soldier goes one step further than the snake: She makes rational judgments and can will to act accordingly. Thus, there is clearly a gradation of souls wherein not every living thing partakes in every power in order to be alive. The rational powers belong exclusively to humans, while the *sensitive powers*—those powers of sensory experience—belong to all animals.

Aquinas's commentary on the vegetative and locomotive powers is irrelevant to our larger conversation. Since they are common to all (or most) souls, these two powers do not pertain to Man as a *person*. We are mostly concerned with considering those powers that relate to personhood, culminating in the rational power. However, it is important to understand how the body and the senses feed the mind and provide data from which the rational can engage with the world. To this end, we are concerned with those powers which are specifically *cognitive* or *appetitive* (passionate) in their operation. In one sense, we can talk about the cognitive powers and the appetitive powers as *introspective versus outrospective*. They can loosely be categorized as *inward-focused versus outward-focused*, my experience of a thing versus how I act upon or react toward that thing.

The three powers of the soul concerned with these two operations are the sensitive, appetitive, and rational (intellectual) powers. The sensitive powers of the soul deal directly with the exterior world and are generally not different from the powers of the animals. The same is true of appetitive powers, in a limited sense: even animals desire, feel distress, etc. By contrast, the rational powers of the soul—reason (intellect) and will—are only present in humans. Through our established story, we shall examine each of these powers.

The Sensitive Powers

The dual operation of the sensitive powers is nearly seamless. The sensitive powers are made up of the five external senses (sight, smell, etc.) and the four interior senses: "'‘common sense, phantasy, imagination, and the estimative and memorative powers.'"[77] The five external senses work together with the interior senses to integrate images into an object of perception (common sense), and to retain those images (imagination, phantasy, or sensory memory). The soul evaluates the object as beneficial or harmful to oneself (estimative power) and, finally, works to retain those evaluations

---

77. Aquinas, *Summa Theologiae,* q. 78, art. 4, *sed contra.* For clarity, it must be noted that reading Aquinas here shows that he, in fact, lists five interior senses according to Aristotle in *De Anima,* but Aquinas equates two of these senses with each other (phantasy and imagination) so that really there are only four: "The 'phantasy' or 'imagination' is appointed; which are the same, for phantasy or imagination is as it were a storehouse of forms received through the senses" (q. 78, art. 4).

of the estimative/cognitive power (memorative power, estimative memory).

Both humans and animals share in all aspects of the sensitive powers, with the notable qualified sharing of the *estimative* power. Strictly speaking, humans do not have an *estimative* power so much as they have a *cogitative* power. It is a subtle difference, but important. Whereas an animal encounters an object with a simple registration (or estimation) of good or evil, humans do *not* encounter the world with a simple registration. The cogitative (estimative) power in humans is directly linked with intellectual power: Humans can detect complex and conflicting goods, as well as the *highest* good for themselves. What is more, humans can choose or reject one or another good they encounter in a single object. Therefore, the first difference we find between animal and human souls is a small but important difference in the sensitive powers of the soul.

Let us illustrate the sensitive powers of the soul using our example. The rattlesnake was out at night, avoiding the heat and presumably hunting. Though a snake is cold-blooded, too much heat can cause it bodily problems. In addition, a snake's typical mammalian prey (such as mice) are more active at night during the warm summer months. Thus, instinct and physical constraints prompted this particular snake's nocturnal romp.

Whereas the dark does nothing to a rattlesnake's senses (its eyes see thermal more than anything else, its sense of smell from its tongue remains undeterred, it still touches, hears, etc.), some of the soldier's five external senses were drastically changed by the dark. The soldier's eyes were unable to detect the snake at first, and the snake's proximity to the building created an echo that caused her ears difficulty in pinpointing the snake's location. This is a rudimentary illustration of how the environment affects the sensitive appetitive: The data perceived by these two subjects' senses was somewhat influenced by the darkness, to the extent that their respective senses were more or less adapted to function in that environment.

The data perceived by the five external senses was immediately communicated to the four internal senses, allowing both the soldier and the rattlesnake to have a coherent image of the experienced situation. First, the data was registered by their brains and transferred to an object of perception by each of their common sense. For the soldier, the initial data would have been the sound of a rattle, followed by a limited visual of the snake's white section just before the rattle began. For the snake, this would be the sound of the door opening, the smell of a human, and the thermal registration of a human shape.

Next, the imagination used this data to retain the images translated by the common sense. Neither the rattlesnake nor the soldier needed to continue experiencing the encounter in order to know the other was there. What is more, both the soldier and the rattlesnake were able in some limited way to *recognize* the other—even though the soldier had never encountered a rattlesnake before, and the snake may or may not have encountered humans before. This would be possible by the soldier having prior exposure to things that make up a rattlesnake: she would already know that a rattlesnake rattles, crawls along the ground, etc. For the snake, the recognition is something more along the lines of a "big thing larger than my food chain, which may or may not know I'm here."

Thirdly, both the soldier and the snake used their estimative power to judge the overall risk or relative benefit to themselves that this encounter presented. Here again, both the soldier and the snake had a similar overall judgment: potential, imminent harm to themselves posed by the other subject.

Finally, all the preceding data, imaging, and estimation that this encounter presented was logged away in the memory of both subjects, further informing future encounters of a similar nature.

This last (the memorative power) was already a factor in both the soldier's and the snake's initial assessments, as well as in the circumstances surrounding the encounter. The soldier knew from prior experience and exposure that rattlesnakes are venomous, can strike far distances, warn unaware hikers, and are faster than human reflexes. The snake, on the other hand, either by instinct or prior experience, knew all too well the potential danger a being too large to be in its food chain could inflict. Wounded predators often starve. And, I would imagine, being stepped on is just not pleasant. As an extended exhibit of the memorative power, the snake had ceased to be surprised by our presence after a while. His recent experience and knowledge that we were in the area caused him to not be fearful when he was transported elsewhere.

These are the operations of the sensitive soul. They work in quick succession with each other and are generally a simple cognition of the situation at hand. The sensitive powers are directly influenced by the external world and the physical makeup of the subject's body. They are overwhelmingly data-driven. We would class the sensitive powers of the soul as *cognitive* powers.

The Appetitive Powers

The second power of the soul we are concerned with is the appetitive. Unlike the data-driven makeup of the sensitive powers, the appetitive powers have no direct access to the outside world. These functions are much more introspective and deal with the subject's *experience* or *reaction* to the encounter. The appetitive powers are split into two operations: the *concupiscible* and the *irascible*. In short, the concupiscible acts with a simple good or evil attitude toward its object: love, hate, desire, aversion, etc. The irascible, on the other hand, acts with complex good or evil toward its object, as when there is some obstacle or difficulty to overcome in accomplishing the object: hope, despair, fear, daring, anger. Again, we turn to our reptilian encounter to understand.

Having obtained a more or less accurate image of the encounter, both the snake and the soldier had an interior movement in light of this data. As already discussed, the immediate reaction of both subjects was negative. Knowing what they did about the actor they were encountering, both the snake and the soldier willed (or intended) to, at the very least, *avoid* the other.

While the snake's specific internal reaction beyond a simple aversion to being stepped on can be up for debate, we can know clearly what the soldier experienced. Whereas the proximity of the snake was clearly communicated by the sound of the rattle, the more specific image of the snake's *location* was initially confused and unclear due to the environmental circumstances. The rattle's sound bouncing off the TOC wall, coupled with the darkness and the relative camouflage of the snake's pattern, led the soldier to experience the rattle as *encompassing*, surrounding her as it were. This, as one can imagine, caused no small amount of distress or perhaps even hatred toward the rattling.

All of these are experiences of an attitude of simple evil toward the object at hand and are illustrations of the concupiscible power of the appetitive. The concupiscible power is directly related to the individual's orientation toward the encountered object, as in, how does this experience relate to my desire *for* this object?[78]

In light of the distress caused by the sense of being surrounded by rattlesnakes, the logical, complex reaction would be one of fear, loss of confidence, and possibly a hint of despair. These reactions all have a further end in mind or an anticipated conclusion to the narrative of the encounter. They recognize the good but elicit an emotive response in the face of a complication in acting upon that good. The soldier initially retreated from the situation. She saw safety as a good but encountered a snake as an obstacle to staying safe and potentially an active threat *to* safety. Thus, fear arose, and she wanted to flee. She lost confidence that she was safe at that time. To remain safe, healthy, and preserve her own existence, she had to change the circumstances.

To be fair, the snake also would have desired to flee the situation (thus demonstrating at least a level of the irascible), but this would be more related to a consequence of the data and a desire not to be stepped on rather than losing confidence that one is safe, so to speak. Thus, the irascible power is more related to

---

78. As an aside, and as a corollary, I happen to love snakes. Thus, when I heard the rattle, the soldier's report of a snake, and saw the snake myself, I was overcome with a sense of *joy*. Simple good towards the snake: I like snakes. Thus, my concupiscible power caused a *good* experience for me.

what a subject wants to *do* in the face of the experience rather than how that experience relates to them as a subject.[79]

Many people describe a rattlesnake that has been surprised as "angry." Though anger is indeed a complex movement (and therefore a movement of the irascible power), I do not think it accurately applies to the snake. This snake was surprised and saw danger, but that would have been pretty much it. Thus, my best stab at the irascible for the snake, in this case, would be fear of being stepped on or perhaps daring in the face of danger.

The concupiscible and the irascible powers of the appetitive do not feed chronologically into one another as straightforwardly as the sensitive powers do. Whereas the sensitive is concerned with the data of the external, the appetitive is concerned with the subject's relation *to* the perceived external. Thus, the soldier and the snake both encountered danger, recognized a general emotive of negative desire for that danger, and experienced an emotive will or intent to flee the scene. Their negative desire for the other subject is a simple evil (concupiscible), while the accompanying fear would be complex (irascible).

---

79. To continue a corollary to the situation, I saw the rattlesnake and fancied a new hatband. The simple good I recognize: "Cool, a snakeskin!" The complication in realizing that good: "The snakeskin is still attached to a live snake." Thus, my irascible power caused a *frustrating* experience for me.

These are the functions that make up the appetitive powers of the soul and, though at times difficult to discern in lower animals, are still largely shared among the animal kingdom. They are internal movements in the face of data. Whereas the sensitive is a *cognitive* power, the appetitive is a *passionate* power.

Aquinas's Rational Powers

The rational (intellectual) powers, unlike the sensitive and the appetitive, move beyond mere experience of the world and are concerned with *understanding*. They are only present in humans. The rational, too, is divided into two operations: the *rational-cognitive* and the *rational-appetitive,* or *reason* and *will,* respectively. In short, these two powers are concerned with understanding the truth of an experience and subsequently acting out the corresponding good in response.

The rational-cognitive (reason) utilizes *ratio* and *intellectus* to make distinctions, determinations, and decisions based on the data provided by the sensitive powers. Reason interprets *what* has been experienced rather than lend itself as *part* of the experience. In other words, the reason acts upon the data already present or actively seeks to obtain further data to behold what or where the good in the incident is. While reason can intuit, expand, or parse out data to make a decision, it does not *provide* any data, emotion, or reaction *to* the experience. In a way, reason can be described as *piercing the dome* of the pure data world (see Chapter I).

By contrast, the rational-appetitive (will) seeks to *live out* what has been determined by the reason. Its aim is to make what is seen as good a reality or to understand and experience the good. The will thus does not behold or account for the object itself in response to data as much as it concerns itself with the good in light *of* the data, instructed by reason. Thus, whereas the other appetitive powers are concerned with the incident's benefit or harm and the subject's response (such as fear or hope), the will is concerned with acting upon what is *actually* good, regardless of the raw consequences of data.

To see this more proximately, we will consider the soldier again. When she encountered the rattlesnake but experienced how hard it was to see, she immediately retreated back into the TOC: She knew that it is *good* to not get bitten, and the way to make that a reality is to retreat. The raw data could have indicated some other action (freezing, running across the field, etc.), but the *actual* good was to retreat inside.

Further, the soldier recognized that the snake posed not only a danger to herself but also to the rest of her unit. Thus, she announced the snake's presence to the next soldier in line (myself) to address the situation. Reason told her that it is *good* that the unit remains safe and free from snakebites; her will caused her to tell the shift NCO about the snake *so that* this recognized good could become a reality and, therefore, be experienced *as* reality.

Aquinas's Body-Soul Composite

Every operation of our being requires a movement of the body, whereupon we then make decisions and direct our will to act upon the physical world. For Aquinas, as in Aristotle, all knowledge comes first through an experience with the outside world, requiring the five physical senses. The mind accepts the experienced reality and begins to abstract and interpret. The memory weighs the experience against other prior experiences, allowing the intellect to make a final determination and interpretation on the merit of the experience and direct a course of action. Finally, the will acts toward what it deems good according to what the intellect has interpreted through the senses.

All of the three preceding powers we have dealt with are concerned with either the cognitive or appetitive movement of the soul. For higher animals, the more rational (cognitive) orders the less rational (appetitive) and the rest of the soul. Thus, in the highest animals (humans), the intellectual powers order every other power. Parsed out more specifically, the appetitive—focusing on my reaction toward a thing—will always proceed *from* the cognitive: I cannot act upon a thing unless I first experience it. Thus, memory of a rattlesnake's danger proceeds *from* encountering or having knowledge of a rattlesnake. Likewise, fear of a rattlesnake proceeds *from* experiencing an aversion to the snake. And finally, reporting the snake to the shift NCO proceeds *from* knowing that, for the sake of the entire unit's safety, it is not good for a snake to be so close to the TOC.[80]

All this being said, experience demonstrates the sensitive appetites can overcome the rational. Many times, "a man's desires [can] violently prevail over his reason, he reviles himself, and is angry at the violence within him."[81] To continue our example from above, what if, instead of retreating from the snake, the soldier had impulsively tried to stomp on its head? We will imagine this fictional alternate course of events in our narrative to explore this.

It requires no imagination to suppose that stomping on the snake's head *could* have been a real impulse for our soldier in question. I must confess, that thought definitely would have crossed my mind. Now, there

---

80. Worthwhile to mention is that Aquinas says there are multiple ways that we can say the powers are ordered. For example, since all knowledge comes through the senses, in the order of origination, it is actually the *vegetative* powers that come first. These allow the possibility for the sensory powers, and only *then* can the rational proceed. It is only in the order of cause (governing or perhaps informing) that we can say the higher orders the lower. Again, there is entirely too much on this topic to tackle in our present discussion. We must continue, having only the limited treatment of this topic.

81. Plato, *The Republic,* 164.

could be many reasons for the soldier's supposed impulse to stomp instead of flee, as there are more irrational powers in the body than there are rational. In this case, we will assume that this impulse was caused by an overwhelming fear that the snake would outrun her and preemptively strike before she could retreat into the TOC.

To be fair, rationally, this fear *could,* in fact, have become reality. Snakes are faster than human reaction speed and have a great striking distance. Thus, in this fictional narrative, the soldier recognizes the snake, experiences the distress that being surrounded by the rattling sound elicits, and immediately jumps out onto the snake's reared head when she finally sees the body. Her fear blocks out any other alternative as she is blinded by a supposed impending strike, and she acts accordingly.

Admittedly, this particular snake *could* have been ornery and looking for a bite of soldier. However, reason clearly suggests that immediately retreating would, in all likelihood, discourage the snake from striking by removing its target. Thus, if reason were to lead and guide the lower powers, retreating back into the TOC would have been her choice. In our fictional example, then, the cognitive is violently overcome by the appetitive, causing the soldier to act irrationally.

This fictional case notwithstanding, even in cases of the lower powers rebelling against the higher, the intellect cannot be *shut off*; the rational still informs all actions at some level or other. Even jumping on the snake's head is done because there is some semblance of reason, making it appear as the best course of action—even if that semblance of reason is implicit, reactionary, and wrong.

Pragmatic experience seems to take issue with the assertion that "the rational informs all actions at some level or another." Surely, we all have several ready examples in our mind wherein we can recall some human or another acting in utter rashness. To all external appearances, these individuals seem to have their reason entirely overcome, acting in such a way that we cannot *help* but describe their behavior as "stupid." Nonetheless, there is an ordering to the powers of the soul wherein, in some way, the higher *does* inform the lower. In the order of nature, "The intellectual powers are prior to the sensitive powers; wherefore they direct them and command them. Likewise, the sensitive powers are prior in this order to the powers of the nutritive soul."[82] Our discussion on knowing something by its telos can help in this matter.

The powers of the soul are each for the sake of allowing the subject to operate and engage in the world according to its nature. Now, humans are *rational animals,* and by nature encounter the world through the lens of reason. Because of this, we can say that, "The senses are for the sake of the intelligence, and not the other way about. The senses are a certain imperfect

---

82. Aquinas, *Summa Theologiae,* q. 78, art. 4.

participation of the intelligence; wherefore, according to their natural origin, they proceed from the intelligence as the imperfect from the perfect."[83] Since in the order of nature, the senses are participants in the intellect, the intellect cannot be entirely *shut off*, as in have no consequence, no part of forming, and no bearing on something even as immediate as a reaction. This is especially true in regard to actions and decisions pertaining to the moral order.

A previous point in our discussion was that *anamnesis* is a form of knowledge, placing it as an attribute of the intellectual powers (but not *one* of the rational powers, any more than *ratio* is a power). Man is *always* invited to recognize God through the created reality, and thereby, in one way or another, can *always* know the good and will it. Conscience prohibits us from never having known fundamental aspects of what is good according to natural and divine law, and we always act toward what we *think* is good. Conscience continues to whisper to the person, even if their lower powers rebel and overcome the higher. And, because conscience continually informs the intellect and orients the actor toward what is perceived as good, the will is therefore inclined to direct action toward the knowledge of what is true.

But it is not enough to abstractly know or think the good; a thing is perfect only "to the degree that it is

---

83. Aquinas, *Summa Theologiae,* q. 78, art. 4.

in act, and imperfect insofar as it is in potency."[84] The choice to act is a property of the will. If we "choose" to act on the intellectual level but do not translate this to real life, we have done nothing but wish. The epistle of James testifies to the relevancy of this for salvation: "And if a brother or sister be naked, and want daily food: And one of you say to them: Go in peace, be ye warmed and filled; yet give them not those things that are necessary for the body, what shall it profit? So faith also, if it have not works, is dead in itself."[85] The first principle, then, which refutes Plato's belief that the body is just a limitation on the soul to be discarded, is this: It is only through the body that we are able to act and, therefore, to experience the good. We will return

84. Chad Ripperger, *Dominion: The Nature of Diabolical Warfare* (Keenesburg, CO: Sensus Traditionis Press, 2022), footnote 7, 2.
85. James 1:5–17 (Douay-Rheims).

to the relationship between the conscience, the will, and the body in Chapter III.[86]

---

86. There is simply too much on this matter to cover in our current project, though in Chapter III, we do tackle more in-depth the problem of setting aside the conscience. As a function of the rational powers, in one sense, the conscience can *never* be set aside and continues to have an influence on individual actions. However, as we will see, the conscience *can* be ignored and formed erroneously such that it is all but silenced. In this way, it *is* possible to say that the conscience "can be laid aside" (Aquinas, q. 79, art. 13).

Here, again, it is worthwhile to remember and note the specific distinction between *conscience* and *anamnesis*. Generally speaking, we do not make too much distinction between the two in this project, though we make a concerted effort to use the more appropriate *anamnesis* at all times. In truth, *conscience* and *anamnesis* are not synonyms (hence our efforts in precise language). *Conscience,* for Aquinas, is a quality that the soul has. It is something infused and is a practical judgment *of* the good in a particular action. *Anamnesis*, on the other hand, is a *recollection*, or a *memory of* the good. It is the operation in which Man *recognizes* God when he encounters Him. The result is generally the same: Do this because it is good, avoid that because it is evil, but the operation is different. In light of this, it is worth noting that whereas we have presented *anamnesis* as a form of knowledge and speak of it generally in the same sections as *reason*, Aquinas specifically calls the conscience an *act*. This would make the conscience part of the *will*, as in an operation or function whose end is the good understood. We cannot spend too much more time on this distinction since we are generally concerned throughout this project with *anamnesis* and its specific operation rather than conscience more broadly speaking.

These are the powers that make up personhood for Aquinas. Note, again, the requirement of a *body* in Aquinas's dealing with the powers of the soul. It is not a simple casing for the soul: The body is a necessity with its own crucial function in the operations of both knowing and acting for the human person. We do not have infused knowledge. Unlike the angels, who are pure spirit, humans do not come to full knowledge (with *intellectus* knowledge) simply by directing our faculty of understanding and our will upon an object. If we cannot act with the body, we cannot experience, encounter, or personally *know* the good; only a theoretical knowledge would be available to us.[87]

Wojtyła

Aquinas defines the powers of the intellect and how they react to the lived experience in order to reach the truth (its true end). Foundational as his work is, Aquinas does not adequately address the problems of subjective experience as presented by modernity. The absurd premise of denying objective reality was simply not a serious thought during his time. A key figure in

---

87. Aquinas deals with this question at length in question 89, The Knowledge of the Separated Soul. It is a difficult question since, up to this point, we have spent so much time demonstrating that all knowledge for humans comes through the senses, and it is a good illustration of one way in which the resurrection from the dead is an essential part of Man's nature and the salvation story.

discussing personhood in relation to objective experience in the face of objective reality is Karol Wojtyła.

Wojtyła discusses the person's *subjective experience* with the reality surrounding him in positive terms, bridging the gap between Thomistic thought and modernity. For Wojtyła, the subjective experience is the *premise* within which each individual of the human species exists. He firmly holds that personhood cannot be boiled down to pure consciousness, nor can it be reduced to a mere internal response to external stimuli. He writes:

> It is true that a human person's contact with the world begins on the "natural" and sensual plane, but it is given the form proper to man only in the sphere of his interior life. Here, too, a trait characteristic of the person becomes apparent: a man does not only intercept messages which reach him from the outside world and react to them in a spontaneous or even purely mechanical way, but in his whole relationship with this world, with reality, he strives to assert himself, his 'I,' and he must act thus, since the nature of his being demands it.[88]

This constitutes only a subtle difference from Aquinas, but an important one.

---

88. John Paul II, *Love and Responsibility*, trans. H. T. Willetts (San Francisco, CA: Ignatius Press, 1993), 23.

In his essay *Person and Community*, Wojtyła speaks of the dangers of equating personhood with consciousness alone as in a vacuum by itself and on the dangers of seeing the person as isolated from both reality and from other persons. The mind and the consciousness of the person are not within a windowless box, isolated from the outside world. Nor are consciousness or intellect powers existing for their own sake. Rather, the subject, in his individual experience of reality, is never alone, even though that person can be the *only one* with that particular experience. He writes:

> When I construct an image of the person as subject on the basis of the experience of the human being, I draw especially upon the experience of my own self, but never in isolation from or in opposition to others. All analysis aimed at illuminating human subjectivity have their 'categorical' limits. We can neither go beyond those limits not completely free ourselves from them, for they are strictly connected with the objectivity of experience. As soon as we begin to accept the notion of "pure consciousness" or the 'pure subject,' we abandon the very basis of the objectivity of the experience that allows us to understand and explain the subjectivity of the human being in a complete way—but then we are no longer interpreting the real subjectivity of the human being.[89]

89. John Paul II, *Person and Community: Selected Essays*, trans. Theresa H. Sandok (New York, NY: Lang, 2008), 222.

Wojtyła certainly admits that the senses can sometimes falter in their dealing with the outside world. However, because of the intimate union between body and mind, he insists that the subjective experience of reality through the senses does *itself* count for some importance, not just as a measure of how accurately they depict reality. For Wojtyła, as with Aquinas, personhood can never be divorced from the lived experience of the individual, nor can it be reduced to the consciousness of that being.

To be clear, Aquinas does not *discount* the importance of the lived experience of Man. He agrees with Aristotle that all knowledge must come through the senses; Aquinas merely does not consider the subjective lived experience of the individual itself to be, in a sense, a *reality* in itself. However, the subjective experience of reality is the first moment of contact between the human person and God. All of creation is, as put by Augustine in *De Trinitate*, the *Vestigia Trinitatem.* It is the footsteps of God, His fingerprints pointing us toward Himself. Creation, then, is the gradual self-manifestation of God to His creatures. His footprints in the experienced world pervade everything the five senses touch.

Augustine describes creation specifically in this light in one of his sermons. He writes,

> Some people, in order to discover God, read a book. But there is a great book: the very appearance of created

> things. Look above and below, note, read. God whom you want to discover, did not make the letters with ink; he put in front of your eyes the very things that he made. Can you ask for a louder voice than that?[90]

If we are to accept this as truth, then the individual, lived experiences of the unique person *must account for something themselves,* as a sort of minireality, not insomuch as whether they accurately depict the *data* to be had in the experienced object, but only insofar as they truly represent what the individual person is experiencing as the first encounter with God through their senses.

90. Augustine, *Sermones,* 68.

The Image of God in Man

As Christians, we believe that Man is created in the image and likeness of God. Though this is a precept of our Faith, we found secular proof for this truth in our brief discussion of Plato's tripartite soul. We now come to the point where we must ask: What attribute specifically is it that constitutes the image of God in Man?

Plato believed that it was by virtue of our reason that we were partakers of the Divine. Aquinas echoes this in question 93, article 3, when he treats the question of angels. Here, he claims that it is by virtue of our rational powers that Man partakes in the image and likeness of God. As a slight qualifier to the claim that Man's reason demonstrates his immortality, *anamnesis,* the knowledge of the good, is seen as constituting the image of God by more recent writers within the Church as well. Belonging to the rational powers, *anamnesis*, at a minimum, testifies to the immortality of the soul.

As similar as reason is to divine nature, God Himself is not simply rational thought. He is a Being existing in a community of Persons. Because God is community, an inclination *toward* life in community is a natural consequence of sharing His image. Without another person to act upon, *good* versus *evil* becomes mere survival. In a world of isolation, there is neither person to behold nor to reveal oneself to.

The image of God within Man leads us to conclude that the "state is a creation of nature, and that Man is by nature a political animal [capitalization mine]."[91] He most fully participates in the image and likeness of God through his capacity, both as an individual and as a species, to live in *community* with another person who is at once of the same substance but is intrinsically *other* than himself. Such a community, when bound together in total communication of self-gift in love, elevates Man to a participating role in the cosmos as a cocreator with God Himself.

---

91. Aristotle, *Politics,* in *The Basic Works of Aristotle*, ed. Richard McKeon (New York, NY: Modern Library, 2001), book 1, chapter 2, 1253a, Kindle.
The translation by Ernest Barker renders this passage as saying: "Man is by nature an animal intended to live in a polis."

Implicit Conscience in Greece

Man as a *conscious* being, with some level of intuitive knowledge, is the first experience of reality the mature mind perceives. This is the most fundamental principle of knowing personhood and of perceiving the immortality of the soul. Plato argues as much in the *Phaedo*, where Socrates is speaking with Cebes in the hours before Socrates's death.

In the *Phaedo*, Plato specifically argues that the theory of knowledge as recollection "necessarily implies a previous time in which we learned that which we now recollect. But this would be impossible unless our soul was in some place before existing in the human form." After a brief recap of his arguments for knowledge as recollection, he concludes "that the soul is in the very likeness of the divine, and immortal, and intelligible, and uniform, and indissoluble, and unchangeable."[92]

Though he does not specifically describe *conscience*, it is clear that for Plato, rational thought alone is not enough to suggest immortality. Immortality is evidenced by the soul's innate recognition of what is true, implicitly denoting a form of conscience.

For Aristotle, as with Plato, the inclination toward what the individual thinker perceives to be good is *the* categorizing principle in which the individual subject

---

92. Plato, *Phaedo,* in *The Essential Plato*, trans. Benjamin Jowett and M. J. Knight (New York, NY: Quality Paperback Book Club, 1999), 624.

is both aware of his own existence and is known to be immortal. Aristotle believes our efforts to "make ourselves immortal, and strain every nerve to live in accordance with the best thing in us,"[93] i.e., live according to reason, allow us to see that our, "own being is desirable for each man [and that our own] being [is] desirable because [we] perceived [our] own goodness."[94] For him, this is evidence enough that the soul is indeed immortal. A conscious being in this view is oriented toward preserving his own existence on no other premise than it appears to himself good that he exists.

A being conscious of his own goodness acts toward further goodness, according to Aristotle:

> The conscious being wishes for himself what is good and what seems so, and does it . . . for his own sake (for he does it for the sake of the intellectual element in him, which is thought to be the man himself); and he wishes himself to live and be preserved, and especially the element by virtue of which he thinks. For existence is good to the virtuous man, and each man wishes himself what is good.[95]

---

93. Aristotle, *The Nicomachean Ethics,* in *The Basic Works of Aristotle*, book X, chapter 7, 1177b.
D. P. Chase's translation renders this as "according to the highest principle in us."
94. Aristotle, *The Nicomachean Ethics,* bk. IX, chap. 9, 1170a.
95. Aristotle, *The Nicomachean Ethics,* 1166a.

Aristotle saw the preservation of self not as the preservation of consciousness but as an action oriented toward living according to what is *good.* Knowledge and response in view of the good, then, is the evidence Aristotle uses to conclude that the soul is immortal. Here, too, we see Aristotle omits the word *conscience* specifically. However, the operations Aristotle describes showcase an implicit notion of the attribute we would later call *conscience.*

Conscience in Christianity

The easiest bridge between ancient Greek philosophy and Christian thought is undoubtably to read Aquinas. True to form, Aquinas is very Aristotelian in his own thought. He echoes the idea that it is specifically Man's rational thought and orientation toward the good that denotes him as having an immortal soul.

Aquinas goes one step further, however. For him, the soul is not immortal on its own merit: it can only be immortal in the context of being an image and a likeness of God. He states that it is "manifest that in Man there is some likeness to God, copied from God as from an exemplar,"[96] and that the main point "in which the image chiefly consists [is Man's] intellectual nature [capitalization mine]."[97] And, in case one were tempted to misunderstand him, Aquinas asserts that the

96. Aquinas, *Summa Theologiae,* q. 93, art. 4.
97. Aquinas, *Summa Theologiae,* q. 93, art. 3.

image of God resides in the intellect of *all* human persons—not just Men of good will. The image of God resides "chiefly in this, that God understands and loves Himself . . . [and] Man possesses a natural aptitude for understanding and loving God; and this aptitude consists in the very nature of the mind, which is common to all Men."[98]

Aquinas never mentions *anamnesis* specifically as the image of God. The closest imagery he uses to the imagery we have used is in question 93, article 6: *The End or Term of the Production of Man*. Rather than simply stating the image of God resides in the reason (even if reason most closely resembles God when Man utilizes it to love God), he states that "the image of God is impressed on [Man's] mind; as a coin is an image of the king, as having the image of the king."[99] Though this last quote does not find Aquinas speaking about the orientation toward the *good* at all, we do not need it for our purpose.

Aquinas already described Man's orientation toward the good above. What he *does* do here is describe the Image of God in a sort of recollection fashion: God's image is already imprinted upon our soul from before our birth. The image of God for Aquinas, then, is the ability and inclination that rises from an imprint on our very soul to reflect, understand, and love God.

98. Aquinas, *Summa Theologiae,* q. 93, art. 4.
99. Aquinas, *Summa Theologiae,* q. 93, art. 6.

Recent great theologians have become more explicit in dealing with *anamnesis* and its character upon the soul. Though Pope John Paul II does not use the technical term *anamnesis,* he does specifically state that the "capacity to command what is good and to forbid evil, placed in man by the Creator, *is the main characteristic of the personal subject.*"[100] This principle is central to both his essays and encyclicals.

Cardinal Joseph Ratzinger understands *anamnesis* precisely in this light in his book *On Conscience*. Here, he codifies the word *anamnesis* as a very specific description of conscience, one with certain ramifications.

Ratzinger posits that an individual's simple guilt in the face of rejecting the foundational moral orientation toward the good does not occur within the consciousness simply *because* Man has a spiritual capacity. Rather, the spiritual capacity, in a sense, drags the physical (willing or unwilling) into the realm of the spiritual, only failing in cases of decidedly horrific instances. At which point, the rejection of the good can only be described as an essential sickness within the person.

And yet, even in these monstrous situations, *anamnesis* cannot fail to exist in principle as an imprint upon the immortal soul:

> The feeling of guilt, the capacity to recognize guilt, belongs essentially to the spiritual make-up of man. This

---

100. John Paul II, *Dominum et Vivificantem*, para. 43.

> feeling of guilt disturbs the false calm of conscience and could be called conscience's complaint against my self-satisfied existence. It is as necessary for man as the physical pain that signifies disturbances of normal bodily functioning. Whoever is no longer capable of perceiving guilt is spiritually ill, "a living corpse, a dramatic character's mask," as Görres says, "Monsters, among other brutes, are the ones without guilt feelings. Perhaps Hitler did not have any, or Himmler, or Stalin. Maybe Mafia bosses do not have any guilt feelings either, or maybe their remains are just well hidden in the cellar. Even aborted guilt feelings . . . All men need guilt feelings.[101]

Here, we find that Ratzinger agrees with Aquinas on the image of God as present within all Men regardless of their beliefs or moral actions: All Men have the same foundational inclination toward God. Even peoples in the farthest reaches of the wilderness "are yearning for [the light of the Gospel] in the hidden recesses of their souls . . . [and that they] recognize in the encounter with the word of the gospel that this indeed is what they have been waiting for."[102]

---

101. Joseph Ratzinger, "A Conversation on the Erroneous Conscience and First Inferences," in *On Conscience,* chapter 1.
102. Ratzinger, "Systematic Consequences."

Final Thoughts on Anamnesis

In the previous chapter, we discussed *anamnesis* as a legitimate source of knowledge. In this chapter, we spent our time discussing it as the characteristic that informs us of our own immortality and our existence as beings in the image of God. As we move forward, we must conclude our discussion aimed at defining *anamnesis* and move toward examining its consequences. Here, we sum up *anamnesis* and its operation in the soul before we move on.

We know the truth *actively* through our reason and *intuitively* (on a basic level) through our conscience. We desire to not simply know the truth but to act according to what is true. As Plato says, "No one is satisfied with the appearance of good—the reality is what they seek; in the case of the good, appearance is despised by everyone."[103] We act according to the truth because it is good—at least, we perceive it to be good. Even those who seem to desire what is evil "desire what they suppose to be good when they are really evils."[104]

Aristotle echoes this sentiment at the beginning of the *Nichomachean Ethics.* He asserts that "every art and every inquiry, and similarly every action and pursuit, is thought to aim at some good; and for this reason the good has rightly been declared to be that at

103. Plato, *The Republic,* 255.
104. Plato, Meno, 438.

which all things aim.'"[105] The individual focuses his attentions toward this Chief Good as a response to the movement from the depths of his own interior. This movement is an "echo of a call from God who is the origin and goal of man's life."[106] It is a distant memory, a recognition of what is good and how to act when we encounter it.

Our discussion on knowledge illustrated what it means to say that Man "remembers" knowledge of good. This knowledge is not *obtained* by him, as much as it emanates *from* the inner recesses of his very being. His prior knowledge of the moral order is evidence of Man's immortality, inasmuch as that knowledge of good on such a basic fundamental level is akin (indeed of the same essence as) the innate knowledge of good within the mind of God. Indeed, there is no coherent way to consider rationality and conscience as evidence of Man's immortality outside of participating in the Immortality of God.

For this reason, it is necessary to consider knowledge provided through anamnesis as the defining point of personhood. It is the characterization of individual and unrepeatable subjectivity as it beholds the moral order revealed to that individual by God on a Being-to-being level.

Further, we conclude that it is a necessary function of the will to act toward that which is perceived

---

105. Aristotle, *Nicomachean Ethics*, bk. 1, chap. 1, 1094a.
106. John Paul II, *Veritatis Splendor*, para. 7.

to be good in response to the individual revelation and communication of the objective moral order. Freedom, therefore, lies within the will, because acting toward what the individual perceives to be the good is the will's necessary function. The will also, therefore, bears the moral weight of individual choice.

The Personalistic Norm

We have just discussed how *anamnesis* denotes *personhood,* a unique unrepeatability which requires the subject to move and act in response to the good written upon his heart. In addition, we intimated that personhood results in an orientation toward community, characterized by mutual communication of self and encounter with another person.

At this time, it is appropriate to ask two questions. First, what is the attitude toward another person that *anamnesis* dictates I maintain? And second, what *responsibility* do I have toward another person? The answer to these two questions will inform the remainder of our larger conversation. Both questions can be answered with the same assertion, an imperative which, in the final analysis, is a variation and improvement on the Kantian proposition.

Kant, in the eighteenth century, proposed that we must always act toward another person such that the object of our action (if they be persons) is an end in themselves and not merely an instrument to my own end. There is merit to this imperative, but it ultimately falls short of being complete. And, in this, we cannot blame Kant. In fact, when your starting premise for reality is the absurd ground rules put forth by Descartes and the Enlightenment, the best, highest hope you can dream of is Kantian metaphysics.

But best of the worst does not mean operable in any coherent way, unfortunately. Genius as Kantian philosophy is, given the premises he adhered to, his philosophy simply does not align with reality once the reality of an objective and tangible world is reintroduced.

We cannot explore the Kantian imperative in depth here. Briefly, Kant operated in a philosophical world which accepted the absurdities of radical subjectivism. Every individual, and every individual experience, was, for Kant, insurmountable. Simply put: I am alone in my subjectivity, and I only see the truth or reality through my own subjective senses. There is no *surety* of the truth, since I already know my senses might lie. So, basically, in a nutshell, think living in the Matrix without anyone coming to unplug you. How would you know if the whole reality was a simulation?

We've already dealt with the Enlightenment, abridged though that dealing may have been. However, the absurdities of radical subjectivism raise difficult questions that, while absurd, can be hard to refute. Kant, as I said, did the best that anyone could hope for given the foundational absurdity of the worldview. If the premises of the Enlightenment are true, then the

Kantian imperative allows us to operate *even within that framework* with a view toward the dignity and moral worth of persons. We just assume that they are potentially as right as I am, and that they have a right to pursue their own ends without being an object, end, or being used by me.

The genius of Pope John Paul II was tackling the absurdities of the Enlightenment, gleaning what was worthwhile from its philosophers, and then reframing their solutions to fit within a world corresponding with reality. Put simply, the problem Kant tried to solve was living *as* a subject within a world consisting of *only other subjects*. Pope John Paul II reframes the problem of living *as* a subject within a world consisting of *other subjects in an objective world*. The difference is subtle, but paramount.

Pope John Paul II's premise is not that we are primarily subjects, but that *I, as an individual, am an object*. It means that I exist, that my existence is a fact, and that my existence is not up for discussion—any more than any other fact of the world is up for discussion. We are subjects living within a world of objects. There is no possible way that I am *not* an object of someone else's actions! So, my existence is an objective fact, and others must deal with it, just as I must deal with them within my own "world."

Moreover, just as I, as a subject, have my own ends, am formed by my own individual background, and have my own subjective experience informing my decisions, so too does every other subject have *their* own ends that are different from mine. Their objectivity in the world does not diminish their subjectivity; rather, their subjectivity is *itself* an objective fact.

With *this* important clarification in mind, Pope John Paul II changes the Kantian imperative from simply avoiding regarding another person with a view toward use to be, "whenever a person is the object of your activity, remember that you may not treat that person as only the means to an end, as an instrument, but must allow for the fact that he or she, too, has, or at least should have, distinct personal ends."[107] This rearticulation of the Kantian principle, retooled and fitted to a coherent worldview, "lies at the basis of all human freedoms, properly understood, and especially freedom of conscience."[108] It is the attitude that *anamnesis* demands from us regarding every other subject. Pope John Paul II would refer to this principle as the *personalistic norm.*

Let us explore this a little more, specifically relating it to *anamnesis*.

One most basic "impulse which arises from within,"[109] orienting the person toward the good known by *anamnesis* is the commandment of love from the Gospel. Pope John Paul II writes that, "On the basic, elementary, pre-ethical level [I am called] to experience

---

107. John Paul II, *Love and Responsibility*, 28.
108. John Paul II, *Love and Responsibility*, 28.
109. John Paul II, *Person and Community*, 203.

another human being as another *I*, [to] participate in another's humanity, which is concretized in the person of the other just as mine is in my person."[110]

The fundamental level of interpersonal experience is twofold. On one side, both persons must recognize the unique subjectivity of the person experienced. This initial recognition in turn results in both persons attempting to truly communicate their own personhood to the other. For this foundation to exist, the only appropriate attitude toward another person is one completely devoid of an intent to only *use* the person as an object, either as a means toward an end or for my own pleasure. Anyone "who treats a person as the means to an end does violence to the very essence of the other, to what constitutes its natural right."[111]

A brief description of what we mean by the term *object of use* can be gleaned from Aristotle. In his example, he attests that the good Man in search of true happiness—looking to act upon the good—would never search after something whose nature is simply "merely useful and for the sake of something else. And so one might rather take [contemplation, honor, friends] to be ends; for they are loved for themselves."[112] This much to say, to not regard the other as only an object of use is to regard the other person as more than simply an object from which we gain something else. We are bound

110. John Paul II, *Person and Community*, 203.
111. John Paul II, *Love and Responsibility*, 27.
112. Aristotle, *Nicomachean Ethics,* bk. 1, chap. 5, 1096a.

through personhood to regard each person as a subject, independent and free, to be encountered and loved. At the same time, we must communicate ourselves to them as an independent, free subject.

I have spent a little bit of time clarifying that the personalistic norm does not allow using another subject as the *only* attitude toward that subject. In the modern world, admitting *any* sort of sense of use toward another person may seem harsh and patently false. However, if you admit the world *exists*, and is not merely a conglomeration of my own experience, this objection quickly falls away.

If I exist as an object, then whenever anyone acts toward or upon me, I necessarily *am* the object of their action. If I am trying to recruit an individual into the military, I am, of necessity, trying to get them to fill an empty role the organization needs. The state or country has a need for someone with their particular skill set. This doesn't necessitate *that individual specifically*, but that individual fits the bill.

Within the bounds of the personalistic norm, I am *not* prohibited from trying to get that individual to enlist as an object who can fit the role I need him to fill. What I *am* prohibited from doing, however, is to stop at that end. I must recognize, allow for, and acknowledge that this individual is not merely something for me to fill a role with. Rather, this individual, like me, has his own ends to every action, *including making me the object of his military exploration*.

We must try to find another, more proximate example of what we mean, and indeed there are many instances we could think of which illustrate holding a person merely as an object of use. Perhaps the most readily apparent one is a reductive attitude toward another person's body as a means for either procreation or for sexual gratification. At this level of interaction, we demean ourselves first by not moving beyond the functions of mere sensory reception. Rather than observing the hierarchy of our soul, we engage our will on a level overcome by passion and lust. In such cases, we also act with intent toward beholding the other person merely as a means to that secondary end.

My intent to view another as an object does nothing to the intrinsic dignity of the other person, however. Personhood carries with it an inviolable dignity, recognized or not. Even if one were to move past abstract regard, to physically use another person in a violation of the personalistic norm and exclusively as an object for use, the dignity of that person would still remain. The dignity of the person is not something that can ever be acted upon from the outside.

Some specific examples might be helpful here. We see an *attitude* of use overflowing into *physical* use in many sexual sins, especially when children are involved. Surrogacy, IVF, abortion, the pill (when used for contraceptive reasons or without grave cause), and rape are grave actions that violate the dignity of the other person. Each one tries in some way to deny a person the recognition their existence deserves. In each event, an actor (for some secondary reason) is intent on gaining some personal end, fulfilling a selfish desire at the expense of some person's body. They take one aspect of the body (or the life) and boil it down to what the *I* wants to get from it with no regard for what the subject in question's aims may or ought to be. Several of these actions go further still, altering or even ending human life, such that the person involved cannot experience reality or act toward what is actually good. They patently deny any right of the other to have any subjectivity whatsoever.

Violation and denial do not alter reality, however. The dignity of the human person remains intact, despite being subjected to use. For this reason, it is not even permissible to treat violent actors in a way that denies their personhood or treats them as mere objects. In circumstances requiring intervention or doling out justice, "reciprocity in accordance with a proportion and not on the basis of precisely equal return [is required]. For it is by proportionate requital that the city holds together."[113]

This principle, then, is the elementary truth of objective morality regarding persons. The personalistic norm "lies at the basis of all the human freedoms . . . especially the freedom of conscience."[114] Its claim can be summed up very shortly. The personalistic norm de-

113. Aristotle, *Nicomachean Ethics,* bk. 5, chap. 5, 1132b.
114. John Paul II, *Veritatis Splendor*, para. 49.

mands "that a person, unlike all other objects of action, which are not persons may not [only] be an instrument of action."[115]

Inclination Toward Community Bound by the Personalistic Norm

As a rational being, Man is inclined toward acting with a mind for the good. This is not his only natural inclination, however. Man experiences several natural inclinations, according to his nature. One of these is a need for community.

Anamnesis orients the person toward a community that actively promotes a regard for persons in accordance with the personalistic norm. The personalistic norm is more than simply the rubric we allow to inform our accidental street meetings; it is the norm used to mold the communities we build.

We cannot treat in depth the nature of Community and Man's social nature in this book. However, our discussion on *anamnesis* as orientation toward foundational truths leads us to introduce it briefly here.

Need for society is, according to Fr. Chad Ripperger, the *third* category of natural inclination in beings. The first two inclinations, preserving one's own existence and fulfilling basic functions associated with life, are shared by all living creatures. *Need for society* is

---

115. John Paul II, *Love and Responsibility*, 27–28.

a category of inclination specific to creatures of the higher order, those with intellect. He writes:

> The third category [of natural inclination] is something specific to man alone who has reason. The natural law also inclines man to live in society and to get along with others. It inclines man toward pursuing the truth and to pursue the truth about God. This would include things such as living in a community which is clear from the fact that they have the ability to communicate.[116]

This conclusion is based on the principles discussed in teleology. Since the end of communication is relation with another person, we know from its end that Man is intended toward community.

Man is not the only *rational* creature, nor is he the sole inheritor bearing the image of God. Though he may be the only *animal* with communal inclinations, Man is not the only *creature* with this bent. Angels, too, are persons themselves, endowed with rational intellect. As such, they also have the inclination to live in community, evidenced by their ability to communicate with each other:

> One does not communicate in isolation but only within the context of a community. Furthermore, [angels] would have a natural inclination to

116. Ripperger, *Dominion,* 28.

> communicate the truth because of the very structure of their minds receiving knowledge directly by the infusion by God . . . their intellect has a natural inclination to know the truth about particulars and a natural inclination to automatically recognize the truth of them . . . Since angels can recognize right from wrong or what is moral and what is immoral, what is sinful and what is not sinful, this means that angels have a conscience.[117]

Anamnesis and teleology both inform us that personhood and the personalistic norm necessarily result in a level of community with another. The resulting community serves as a unifying principle between two (or more) persons by virtue of interaction and action by the individuals involved, appropriate to their role in relation to each other.

Angels and Men both share in the image of God. This fact at first suggests that there is therefore nothing special about Man in the cosmos. Man is outdone even in his own right as a rational creature. This is not the case, however. Our discussion on epistemology requires us to say one thing specifically concerning the community of Man, as he is a body-soul composite. We premise this observation on the *second* of the four natural inclinations, articulated by Aquinas and referenced by Ripperger. We already discussed the third (inclination toward community). We will not expound

117. Ripperger, *Dominion*, 28–29.

upon the first and fourth at this time; only the second one concerns us here, i.e., the inclination toward the natural functions of one's being.

Man is endowed with a body. As such, the natural functions of his being are those common to the higher *animals*: eat, reproduce, etc. Though the inclination toward acting upon the natural functions of being is shared with all animals of the higher order, actions performed by the human person take on a special character—even actions of common function with lower animals. Even the human fulfillment of physical drives is guided by reason.

Reason alone as an isolated, abstract function does not elevate human action, however. In one sense, there is personhood in the body, not independent from the spiritual, rational, element, but rather as an integrated requirement for the person to be whole. Man *exists* without the body to be sure; however, he cannot act or will or, properly speaking, even reason without his body.[118] The body is a requirement to function for Man.

Unlike the angels, Man needs his body to communicate. Angels do not have bodies; they communicate with each other through pure intellect and will. Where angels have complete knowledge of what another person manifests to them in an instant, Man can only come to any knowledge of the other through his senses. As a result, Man requires the use of his body to communicate, manifest, and give himself to the other person.

---

118. See Footnote 87

In a larger discussion, it would be appropriate to mention that the total gift of oneself is an important part of communicating oneself to another. That is outside the scope of epistemology, however. Here, we must content ourselves to pointing out how God has tied the self-gift aspect of Man's communication to the sexual act. Whereas in animals, the natural inclination to reproduce is restricted to the instinctual function of being, in Man, it has the "natural tendency to develop into love simply because the two objects affected, with their different sexual attributes, physical and psychological, are both people. Love is a phenomenon peculiar to the world of human beings. In the animal world, only the sexual instinct is at work."[119]

For Man, an *act of intimacy* is not mere reproduction; it is a total gift and revelation of the self, incorporating the whole of the body and creating the bond of full knowledge and love between two humans. The second inclination in Man is, through love, really elevated to a function of the third kind, fulfilling his need for community. The intimacy in this special interaction is the foundation of all societies. It is the primary way Man gives himself in total communication. In the context of the personalistic norm, this particular kind of community between a man and a woman ensures that:

> A person of the opposite sex cannot be for another person only the means to an end—in this case sexual pleasure

119. John Paul II, *Love and Responsibility*, 49.

> or delight. The belief that a human being is a person leads to the acceptance of the postulate that enjoyment must be subordinated to love. 'Use,' not only in the first, broader and objective meaning, but also in its second, narrower, more subjective meaning (for the experience of pleasure is by its nature subjective), can be raised to the level appropriate to an interpersonal relationship only by love. Only 'caring' precludes 'using' in the second sense, as well as the first.[120]

120. John Paul II, *Love and Responsibility*, 34.

Concluding the Human Person

Man is both mortal and divine. He is mortal by virtue of his body, divine by virtue of his reason. Within the tripartite soul of Man lies the powers which make up the functions of the intellect, orient the passions, and inform the will. *Anamnesis*, existing as "the love of God [which is] not founded on a discipline imposed on us from outside, but is constitutively established in us as the *capacity* and *necessity* of our rational nature,"[121] instructs him to act toward the good. This orientation toward the good is the specific attribute that imprints the image of God on the soul of Man. The basis for the dignity of human life is just this: that Man is an individual subject, created in the image of God.

121. Monastic rule of St. Basil, italics mine.

Upholding the dignity of the person goes one step further than merely allowing them to exist. We must avoid any sense of mere *use* of the person in relation to ourselves and encounter persons as unique, unrepeatable subjects with free will, living with a specific experience of God known only to himself. This is the basis of the natural law: It is person-based, aimed at encountering, dignifying, and promoting the life of the person. The natural law is not individualistic but communal in focus, resulting in a necessity for communal life between persons, a community founded on the personalistic norm.

We will discuss natural law in more detail in Chapter III.

Chapter III

Freedom and the Will

"Everyone has his own specific vocation or mission in life; everyone must carry out a concrete assignment that demands fulfillment. Therein he cannot be replaced, nor can his life be repeated, thus, everyone's task is unique as his specific opportunity to implement it." Victor Frankl, (*Man's Search for Meaning, 1959*)

Our discussion thus far has been mainly focused on the *intellectual* functions of Man's soul. Of special interest has been *anamnesis* as the function of the intellect that denotes immortality and personhood. We have seen that *anamnesis* orients the actor toward the good by *recognizing* goodness because, in some way, the good has been imprinted upon Man's soul.

We remember that the tripartite soul is not only intellect but also passions and will. Now, the operation of the passions does not play a *formal* role in our larger discussion. To be sure, they are a necessary movement in the soul. However, space constraints require us to deal only implicitly with the passions, and then again only in relation to reason and the will. Indeed, we explored the operation of the passions briefly in our examples of the sensitive and appetitive powers, according to Aquinas. At this time, we find it necessary to treat the will formally as we launch into the concluding portions of this book.

We have, at this point, dabbled in the relationship between *recognizing* the good (as a source of knowing what is good) and *acting* toward that good. In this chapter, we examine the necessity of the person to act in response to reason and delve more deeply into *anamnesis* as a knowledge act. Furthermore, we will discuss the concept of freedom and why it is a necessary attribute of the will. We will contemplate the moral significance of individual actions themselves versus the moral significance attributed to actions, influenced by the intentions or relative innocence of the actor. To understand the more modern definition of freedom, we will explore the contrasting viewpoints of Ockham and Pinckaers.

The Form and Telos of the Will

The starting point of knowledge is an experience of the world through the senses. The mind accepts the world as presented through the senses, abstracts the experience, and begins to interpret it. Finally, the memory recalls prior similar experiences, enabling the intellect to form a final judgment and interpretation regarding the relative merit (good, bad, pleasant, etc.) of the experience. We explored this operation in the previous chapter through our story of the soldier and the snake.

The will acts as a response to the knowledge *perceived* by the senses, *abstracted* by the intellect, and *oriented* by the conscience. The information obtained in this process informs the will and inclines it toward an appropriate course of action. In this case, *appropriate* means a response or intention oriented toward what the subject perceives to be good at this particular time. The subject thus acts "according to the right rule"[122] when he performs this process without having his reason "ruined by pleasure or pain."[123] This is the operation whereby the subject makes determinations according to his reason.

The operations just recounted direct us toward a deeper examination of the will and its direct relation to *anamnesis*. For its part, *anamnesis,* we remember, is a form of knowledge, an "impulse which arises from within."[124] It is the intelligible proof of Man's immortality, and because of this, the form of *anamnesis* is undeniably immaterial.

We know the *function* of *anamnesis* from a prior discussion, namely, that *anamnesis* orients and reminds the subject on a fundamental level of what is good. Hence, causing the subject to recognize the good and helping him to desire to act upon it is the telos of *anamnesis*. As the telos of *anamnesis* involves motivating the subject to act toward the good, we must examine the *acting* operation of the soul, more broadly

---

122. Aristotle, *Nichomachean Ethics,* bk. II, chap. 2, 1103b. D. P. Chase's translation renders this as the subject acting in "accordance with Right Reason."
123. Aristotle, *Nichomachean Ethics,* bk. VI, chap. 5, 1140b. D. P. Chase renders this as not having been "corrupted by reason of pleasure or pain."
124. John Paul II, *Person and Community,* 203.

speaking. The will of Man is the function of the soul driving such action.

The form of the will is spiritual and belongs to the higher powers. Aquinas places the will as a movement of the soul with a proximate relation to the intellect. He claims that "the good understood is the object of the will,"[125] thereby demonstrating that the form of the will is within the rational realm. The power of the will is tied to the very identity of the individual person.

The previous quote from Aquinas also gives a concise articulation of what we may consider to be the telos of the will: an understanding of the good. But *understanding* is the object of knowledge, and all knowledge comes through the senses. Therefore, the person's senses cannot be discarded as superfluous to either the person or the functions of reason.[126] Consequently, understanding the good requires physically acting upon what is seen as good. The subject is always moved to *act* in response to the good, as perceived by the intellect.

---

125. Aquinas, *Summa Theologiae,* q. 82, art. 4, "I answer that."

126. See footnote 80, on the different ways the powers of the soul can be thought to be ordered. In the order of governance, the irrational proceeds *from* the rational; however, in the order of chronology, the rational proceeds *from* the irrational (i.e., though reason guides the senses, reason can have no access to data or the world without the senses first experiencing this data).

This is not to say the actor in question is moved by necessity, as in a compulsory action upon the best good the intellect perceives. *Anamnesis* is not a raw, compulsory instinct, nor is the will an automatic reaction toward any such instinct. The will desires the good, inasmuch as what is good makes the person happy: "All desire happiness with one will."[127]

Now, any given action could offer varying levels of happiness: false happiness, temporary pleasure, existential fulfillment, etc. In the face of nearly infinite variations of apparent desires, only one remains constant: Each individual actor's will "must of necessity adhere to the last end, which is happiness."[128] This much to say, the will always chooses to act upon *some* apparent good or other as offering *some* form of happiness or other. We will flesh this out a bit more.

Adhering to and acting upon the good is not a passive, deterministic result such as occurs in chemical reactions or at the conclusion of a geometric proposition. The individual is not "forced [to act] by some agent, so that he is not able to do the contrary."[129] This would be *necessity by coercion,* i.e., the individual necessarily must act so because some outside force has exerted sufficient power upon him, rendering him powerless to do anything other than what the stronger force determines. On the contrary, the will necessarily chooses

127. Augustine, *De Trinitate*, xiii, 4. Page 109.
128. Aquinas, *Summa Theologiae,* q. 82, art. 4.
129. Aquinas, *Summa Theologiae,* q. 82, art. 1.

the good on account of the will's orientation toward the good by an "intrinsic principle . . . [which is called] 'natural' and 'absolute necessity.'"[130]

Moreover, the will (being a power and of the same nature as the faculty of reason) *chooses* some goods over others; what is "good is of many kinds, for this reason, the will is not of necessity determined to one."[131] We sometimes call these *conflicting goods*.

When confronted with conflicting goods, the will chooses only that good which seems best. Such is the case when a group of young boys disregards their parents' directive to remain dry and chooses to go swimming in the nearby river instead. Enjoying nature, swimming, camaraderie, beating the heat, and playing are all goods in themselves. But so are obedience to parents, avoiding potential pathogens that could be in the water, not inviting snake or alligator bites, and minimizing the risk of drowning.

Now, the boys in question certainly do not rationally measure all of these possibilities and explicitly choose only the good that seems best to them. However, it must be said that in this case, for one reason or another, *swimming* presents itself to their minds as somehow better, more good, and bringing more ultimate happiness than obeying their parents would have.

In almost any choice, there are, or at least seem to be, two or more conflicting goods. Nonetheless, the

---

130. Aquinas, *Summa Theologiae,* q. 82, art. 1.
131. Aquinas, *Summa Theologiae,* q. 82, art. 2.

will can *always* choose what is truly good, regardless of physical constraints or limitations. History provides numerous examples of individuals who were coerced by malicious external forces to ends or purposes beyond their consent or desire. Yet, in a sense, these individuals still retain their freedom. These otherwise compulsed actors continue, on a personal level, to desire and choose (to the best of their ability) goods they are physically restrained from pursuing. In not-so-distant history, an especially clear illustration of humans rising above their environment is present in the horrible atrocities and experiences of the German concentration camps.

The concentration camps offer a stark example of an individual's ability to choose between conflicting goods. These camps presented numerous legitimate desires to those held captive there. Life (existence), pleasure, power, escape, friendship, eating, etc., all present themselves as viable goods that each individual could pursue. Many *did* pursue one or the other of these, to the exclusion of pursuing anything else—and often to the detriment of their fellow captives. Amidst the horrors against human dignity in these environments, a few individuals "managed to [continue to] relate to others as other *I's,* as *neighbors*—often to a heroic degree."[132] These few people did not reduce themselves or their desires to mere fulfillment of bodily passions, but chose to always live according to the

132. John Paul II, *Person and Community*, 206.

personalistic norm. Many died because of their heroism. And so, here we see the first point in our discussion of freedom: The individual person *chooses* one good or another in any particular action, even in the face of physical restraint.

Discussion on the Nature of "The Good" and "Freedom"

At this point in our discussion, it seems appropriate to discuss what is "good." Further, we must ask what exactly is *the "good"* toward which *anamnesis* inclines the person. The good can be said to be of many kinds, and the person is able to choose between several conflicting goods. Therefore, the will is not oriented toward one good, to the exclusion of all others. We are left to wonder what the relation is between the *actual* good versus the *perceived* good, or the *best* good over some inferior goods.

Moreover, if *anamnesis* is a fundamental recollection of the good, intended to orient the subject toward that good by recognizing it in physical experiences, how is it possible some individuals seem to *genuinely* desire and consistently choose that which is objectively *not* good, all with complete interior integrity? What is to be said about the dignity of persons who, in perpetually choosing evil over the good, "sink to the bottom of the lake [of their own sin] so that they can no longer swim out, and [become] 'those [whom] God forgets?'"[133] Such individuals, in their obstinate persistence in evil, thereby commit the unforgivable sin against the Holy Spirit Christ foretold to the Apostles. Since freedom (as a choice to act, desire, pursue one good over another) "is at the heart of our existence,"[134] are we to conclude that these evil-acting subjects are considered less persons than others? We shall discuss these questions in this section.

The Good According to Antiquity

In a modern world, the word *good* can take on an unwarranted connotation of imposed morality. This much to say, many people who speak of what is "good" are, in reality, really speaking of what they think is

---

133. Fyodor Dostoyevsky, "The Grand Inquisitor," in *Notes from Underground and the Grand Inquisitor*, trans. Ralph Matlaw (New York, NY: Plume, 2003), 125, Kindle.
H.P. Blavatsky's translation renders this as those who "sink so low that they no longer can rise to the surface are forever forgotten by God, i.e., they fade out from the omniscient memory."

134. Servais Pinckaers, *The Sources of Christian Ethics*, trans. Mary Thomas Noble (Edinburgh, Scotland: T&T Clark, 2001), 328.

"right" versus what is "wrong," especially as applied to actions.

But classical philosophy never considered the "good" in such terms. Rather, the concept of what is *good* can never be separated from the concept of what *is.* Just as we cannot conceive of a "watch" without reference to a "*good* watch," so too can we not think of a "*good* watch" if there is no watch to begin with. To this end, thinkers who ascribe to the classical understanding of the cosmos hold that *existence itself* is "the first and basic good of every creature . . . all other goods derive from this basic good."[135]

There is a sound internal logic to this conclusion. If a thing does not *exist*, it can neither act nor be acted upon: "I can only act while I *am* [italics mine]."[136] This logic plays out in the various forms of *Cogito, ergo sum,* which have been articulated over the years: If I am thinking about myself and can experience, then I know that I am here. I know that I do, in fact, exist. This is the prime encounter with reality: a recognition of *my* subjectivity in the world, contrasted with others.

Realizing my own existence as the first encounter with reality informs classical philosophy's conclusion that anything "that which is *per se*, i.e., substance, is prior in nature to the relative (for the latter is like an offshoot and accident of being)."[137] It follows that not only

---

135. John Paul II, *Love and Responsibility*, 51.
136. John Paul II, *Love and Responsibility*, 51.
137. Aristotle, *Nichomachean Ethics,* bk. I, chap. 6, 1096a.

is *existence itself* the prime good, but also that which cannot *not* exist is of a higher good or is more perfect than that which can *cease* to exist. In other words, anything relying on something else for its own existence is lesser than that which exists in its own right. So, in the case of the *cogito* in rational thought and the existence of the soul, there is nothing else upon which the existence of the *I* experience depends. Therefore, it exists necessarily because there is no way it *could not* exist. Things that exist of necessity are eternal.

The objective goodness of existence is articulated by Aquinas when he posits, "It is clear that a thing is desirable only in so far as it is perfect; for all desire their own perfection. But everything is perfect so far as it is actual. Therefore, it is clear that a thing is perfect so far as it exists; for it is existence that makes all things actual."[138] Let us consider my personal lot in life as a bald man to illustrate all this: I cannot have hair if I do not exist; my hair depends on *me* for its own existence. Therefore, *I* must be higher in nature than my *hair* (Aristotle's point: that which exists of itself is higher than that which exists dependent on it). It is more important that I *exist* than it is whether I have hair or not.

I exist, but I am bald. It would not be true to posit that by having no hair, I have *perfect hair for me*, for that is really saying perfection for me is to have no hair. This may be true (I *am* dashingly handsome in my

---

138. Aquinas, *Summa Theologiae,* q. 5, art. 1.

baldness), but the hair that I possess would not itself be perfect because *it does not exist.* I might be said, then, to have the perfect *amount* of hair, but not perfect hair (Aquinas's point: Existence makes all things actual, and a thing is only perfect inasmuch as it is actual).

At the beginning of our discussion, we accepted as given that the Christian God exists. We have already based several conclusions premised on God. As such, *proving* His existence is beyond the scope of our discussion. Nevertheless, I would be remiss were I not, in brief passing, to touch upon *existence as good* as one argument for such proof. In short, everything comes about because something else works upon it. Order cannot come from chaos. Because we exist, there must have been something that moved upon us and brought us into existence: There is a mover.

But something cannot create another thing more perfect than itself. Because we see all sorts of perfection within the world, the mover must be first, uncreated (or else there is an infinite regression of movers into an absurdity), and all perfect. Finally, because existence is better than potentiality, this prime mover must be *pure act* and pure intellect.[139] This must conclude our brief aside into proving God's existence.

---

139. For this entire argument, please refer to Book 12 of Aristotle's *Metaphysics.* Aquinas also deals with the concept of the prime mover (in his own way, not exactly the same as Aristotle's) in his five arguments for the existence of God in Question 2 of the *Summa.*

The Chief Good

Man always acts with an "aim at some good"; the good is the necessary end toward "which all things aim."[140] Aristotle's assertion here, accompanied by our discussion thus far denoting existence as the prime good, utilizes language similar to how we described the personalistic norm. The personalistic norm demands that personhood be encountered not through an attitude of *utility* (a means to an end), but as an end in its own right; similarly, Aristotle describes the good as that necessary end which is, in its own right, *the* end which is the intention of action.

The language similarities between the good and the personalistic norm become even more clear in Aristotle's division of the good into two distinct classes. He states that "goods must be spoken of in two ways, and some must be good in themselves, the others by reason of [some further deep-seated desire for a different good]."[141] Here, we can detect goods that are only such inasmuch as they provide us some further good (acting upon them with an attitude of utility) versus another good, which is *the* good in its own right, desired for its own sake. Aristotle's division of goods and the apparent link between goodness and the personalistic norm prompt us to explore specifically the distinction between *a* good and *the* good.

---

140. Aristotle, *Nichomachean Ethics,* bk. I, chap. 1, 1094a.
141. Aristotle, *Nichomachean Ethics,* bk. I, chap. 6, 1096b.

There are multiple ways we can consider something to be *a* good, but we sometimes have trouble distinguishing in our own desires what is *the* good we are really looking for. Pleasure is considered to be good, as is the absence of pain, bodily health, nourishment, fulfilled desires, etc. Each of these, by itself, is a legitimate good toward which an actor may intend. Nevertheless, pragmatic experience demonstrates that desires are not always fulfilled or even sometimes accurately interpreted by the subject. Choices aimed at fulfilling subjective desires sometimes lead to what is, in truth, *contrary* to what is objectively good for the individual. Let us look at an example.

An individual who uses heroin or other narcotics sees these substances as a means toward something else, such as alleviating depression, experiencing euphoria, conquering the effects of withdrawal, etc. These are all, at best, goods for the sake of something else, according to Aristotle's division of the good. However, the negative effects these substances have on the user actually serve to *rob* him of many things he is actually seeking to gain from using. Instead of rising above depression or addressing the effects of withdrawal, frequent substance users actually create *more* addiction, depression, pain, and suffering for themselves. It would seem that the transitive ends, such as alleviating the symptoms of addiction, are not, therefore, *really* the furthest end that the user in this example desires.

Something further, more complete, and long-lasting is disguised and promised *through* these temporary goods.

Aristotle recognized the transitive natures of some goods and desires and set out to categorize the goods, not merely distinguish between them. Through this, he determines to discover what is *the* good, or the highest good. In his view, there must be "some end of the things we do, which we desire for its own sake (everything else being desired for the sake of this), and if we do not choose everything for the sake of something else (for at that rate the process would go on to infinity so that our desire would be empty and vain), clearly this must be the good and the chief good."[142] All other goods toward which an individual might be inclined to choose are only chosen in light of aiming at things only insofar as they participate, to one degree or another, in the Chief Good. That which has an end in itself is what is to be considered the Chief Good, beyond which there can be no further purpose for willing it other than it is *good itself.* This final aim is not *a* good but is *the* good that we have been searching for. And what is this

142. Aristotle, *Nichomachean Ethics,* bk. I, chap. 2, 1094a. D. P. Chase renders this as there being: "some one End which we desire for its own sake, and with a view to which we desire everything else. Since we do not choose in all instances with a further End in view (for then men would go on without limit, and so the desire would be unsatisfied and fruitless), this plainly must be the Chief Good, *i.e.* the best thing of all."

good, further than which no other good can be desired? Simply put, Man wants to be happy.

In every decision, Man's *true* intention is aimed at *happiness*. From this, we can say, "All men desire happiness with one will,"[143] and see it as the Chief Good.

Now, in the course of this discussion, we have listed several different things that beckon to Man, seeming to promise to grant happiness. Pursuing this promise, Man does at times choose to act upon things as if goods in themselves, but which, objectively speaking, are, in fact, harmful to him. Therefore, we can conclude that Man only chooses things that he perceives will give him at least *some* level of happiness.

The ultimate conclusion to this line of thought—which Aquinas would attest to—is that God, who is the prime mover, the first Cause and Existence in Himself, must also, therefore, be the ultimate source of happiness. He Himself, then, is the Chief Good on account of which we act and choose.

The Problem of Evil

A problem arises in talking about the good—we must deal with the concept of *evil*. Our assumption is that there is a God, and in Christian thought, He is all good. However, our experience admits the "existence" of evil. Drug addiction and its disastrous effects have already been mentioned, and many feel its grip. War

143. Augustine, *De Trinitate*, xiii, 4.

touches as many people as ever, and the world seems no closer to peace than it was when Cain introduced it. Birth defects seriously hinder an individual's ability to use their whole body to encounter reality, and death destroys that ability completely. Be it pain, poverty, jealousy, hunger, or something else, every person can attest to evil in their own lives and the lives of their loved ones.

There is no shortage of examples illustrating the universal experience of evil. Therefore, the original assumptions of either God existing or existence by its nature *is* good appear to be erroneous in some way. What is more, the whole concept of intelligible reality comes into question when we begin to examine what the form and the telos of evil might be. Telos presupposes an intelligent creator who creates with a specific purpose in mind. What would be the *purpose* of evil? And why would a good, intelligent Creator design it? To answer these questions, we must turn to Augustine.

The articulation addressing the problem of evil would be one of Augustine's many great contributions to the philosophical conversation. Born of his experiences with Manichaeanism, Augustine sidesteps the "problem" of evil in a sense and paints it as an absurdity with no real place or intelligibility in the world. Anticipating the principle that Aquinas, after him, would articulate as "all being, as being, has actuality and is in some way perfect; since every act implies some sort of perfection; and perfection implies desirability and goodness,"[144] Augustine posits that "evil has no existence except as a privation of good, down to that level which is altogether without being."[145]

In reflecting on the creation of the world, Augustine uses the example of darkness to illustrate the concept of nonexistence and the presence of attributes *not* created by God, who Himself is existence itself and all good. For Augustine, darkness is not *something* in its own right; it does not *exist.* Instead, darkness can only be thought of as an "absence of light. Where, then, light did not yet exist, the presence of darkness was the lack of light . . . just as when there is no sound there is silence, and the place where there is silence, is the place where there is no sound."[146] So, too, is it with evil. *Evil* is not created by God, nor can it *exist* in its own right. It is an absence, a *deprivation of good.*

The only way we can speak of evil is in relation to that which *does* exist. An "evil thing," therefore, can only be thought of as evil inasmuch as there are one or more aspects of good within it that would, though being individually thought of as *goods*, together constitute some particular aspect at that moment which otherwise deprives the actor of the highest good. Augustine writes:

---

144. Aquinas, *Summa Theologiae,* q. 5, art. 3.
145. Augustine, *Confessions*, trans. Henry Chadwick (Oxford, NY: Oxford University Press, 2008), book III, chapter 12, Kindle.
146. Augustine, *Confessions*, bk. XII, chap. 3.

> But in the parts of the universe, there are certain elements which are thought evil because of a conflict of interest. These elements are congruous with other elements and as such are good, and are also good in themselves. All these elements which have some mutual conflict of interest are congruous with the inferior part of the universe which we call earth. Its heaven is cloudy and windy, which is fitting for it.[147]

For Augustine, the presence of evil in the world has neither a form nor a telos in its own right. The form of evil would be some lack or failing within the good thing itself. It is a twisted or inappropriately desired good which, in itself, is still a good—just existing without proper relation to its own true end as a created thing in the real world. There is no telos for such a deficiency: The desire is still for the good, and the existence of the object in question retains its original telos.

Let us use an example to better see the truth about evil. Health is a good because it is that which is created by God. It is the normal order, the correct operation of the body according to its nature. The flu virus is also

---

147. Augustine, *Confessions*, bk. VII, chap. 19.
As an aside, this quote is a great illustration of classical philosophy's goal of beholding the whole of reality as an integrated reality to be encountered and contemplated, aiming not so much at a *ratio* knowledge akin to merely a categorization and listing of reality but a knowledge aimed at *intellectus* and true understanding.

a good. It, too, is created by God and *exists*. Like any properly functioning body, the flu virus is proper to itself and behaves according to its own nature and is, therefore, *good*.

Because the flu virus exists, we can make determinations about its form, and we can come to conclusions about its telos, just as we could about any other existing object (an exercise we will not undertake at this time). However, when the flu virus takes up residence within a human subject, this virus deprives the subject of health and causes illness. *Illness* does not exist; it is merely a consequence we speak of to denote the absence of health caused by one or more conflicting goods in the same space at the same time, which otherwise do not interact in the natural order of the cosmos. Such an absence requires a *response* from a qualified and capable outside actor who can restore that which is absent.

The concept of a Messiah is the central belief in both Christianity and Judaism. Augustine's articulation of what is *evil* demonstrates why a Redeemer is necessary. For him, evil is not intelligible or something to be understood. Rather, evil is a consequence requiring a response. What is absent must be made "re-present" for there to be good, for something to therefore exist. For Christians, this response is the response of the Cross. A good and loving God could not leave His children in a state of nonbeing.

We can follow along our thought process to see our final point in discussing the nature of the good and the happiness toward which our desires are oriented. God is existence, and existence is good. He created us and holds us in being (as known from the principle of the first mover). The Chief Good after which we desire is not merely *happiness*; Man desires happiness with God in heaven. And here, we can see a complete exposition of the personalistic norm as it relates to happiness.

The personalistic norm dictates that personhood be encountered not in utility, or as a means to an end. It demands that each subject be encountered in its own right. Now, what is acted upon for its own sake is happiness, and the highest end is happiness with God. The personalistic norm, therefore, does not *impose* or make *demands* of Man. It is, in reality, the most perfect experience of happiness. In the core of our being, we find not the *imposition of a moral order*; we find an ardent desire *to pursue and observe that order*.

Freedom

Evil can only be thought of as an *absence* of that which is good, which we have already said is happiness with God. Rephrasing the dictates of *anamnesis* in this light, we can thereby know by an "immediate, intuitive character . . . [that] 'good is to be done, and evil avoided.'"[148] *Anamnesis* binds us to actions of *ought* as relates to good and evil. The imperative here is not so much to act toward what appears good to us in any instance (lesser, transitive goods); rather, it binds us to act according to the *highest* good, a good we can only experience through observing the imperative *do good, avoid sin.*

In this way, the dictates of *anamnesis* attach an intrinsic moral weight to the realm usually reserved for religion: that there is within the will a *responsibility* to work toward the good. This moral weight translates to a sense of *duty*, which "itself is a given in internal experience and becomes evident as a distinct fact-phenomenon, as a fact 'in the person' (and at the same time a fact which is constitutive of the person)."[149]

We will return presently to the concept of sin as being an absence of good. At this time, we shall explore what implications a *duty* toward the good holds for our will. Put simply, we must examine the role of freedom in the subject while he endeavors to discern which conflicting good to choose.

We have already determined that *anamnesis* is the power at the foundational level of personhood through which God personally orients the person toward Himself. Likewise, we have spent a good deal of time contemplating the senses as being that power through

148. John Paul II, *Man in the Field of Responsibility* (South Bend, IN: St. Augustine's Press, 2011), 51.
149. John Paul II, *Man in the Field of Responsibility*, 16.

which we encounter reality. Moreover, we have designated physical reality itself as the vestigia of God, intended to interact with the movement of *anamnesis* and bring the subject toward true happiness and the Chief Good, communion with God. Concluding that the senses constitute a unique and unrepeatable experience of the physical world in each subject in a manner that *matters in itself*, we are now prepared to make a preliminary definition of freedom and comment on its role in the will. According to our logical progression, freedom is a principle necessarily present within the subject, enabling him to choose the one good out of multiple conflicting goods encountered simultaneously, which results in the closest communion with God.

Anamnesis orients the subject to seek and recognize an encounter with God. Man, thus, seeks happiness with God and ardently *desires* to reach Him—but he can only do this by living according to the truth. A desire to follow the moral order is, therefore, already present in Man. As such, God's law, as known through the dictates of the moral order, "does not reduce, much less do away with, human freedom; rather, it protects and promotes that freedom." It is a path, a set of goods, that results in the happiness of Man.

Since all Men desire with one will to do good and avoid evil, freedom is not an array of choices among which the subject can decide for himself what he wants. Instead, freedom is the ability to "avoid [evil] without conscious effort . . . This is called *freedom for excellence,* for it enables us to understand and speak with perfection."[150] Freedom for excellence is best seen through the lens of a practical example.

We will consider as our example a child interested in playing the piano. At the beginning of his budding career as a pianist:

> The child . . . will often feel that the lessons and exercises [are] a constraint imposed on freedom and the attractions of the moment. There are times when practice has to be insisted upon. But with effort and perseverance, the gifted child will soon be able to make notable progress and will come to play with accuracy and good rhythm, and with a certain ease—even the more difficult pieces . . . Soon the child is no longer satisfied with the assigned exercises but will delight in improvising. In this way, playing becomes more personal. The child [will begin to play with mastery] . . . whatever may be suggested, playing with precision and originality, delighting all who hear. Further, this artist will compose new works, whose quality will manifest the full flowering of talent and musical personality.[151]

The child, in this instance, moves from a state that impedes his desire (to play the piano) to a state where he can exercise true freedom. His increased freedom

---

150. Pinckaers, *The Sources of Christian Ethics*, 356.
151. Pinckaers, *The Sources of Christian Ethics*, 355.

results in the complete realization and enjoyment of his personal happiness, allowing him to act unhindered toward what makes him happy.

The child only embodies true freedom *through repeatedly choosing an action that corresponds directly to the final end of his desire already present in his heart, that is, what most directly corresponds to* and influences his ability to play the piano. Note the initial inclination *toward* playing music, which already resides within the child: It is a *gifted* child we are speaking about.

The freedom and skills that come with playing the piano do not stem from the *mere* repetition of the exercises his teacher inflicts upon him. Freedom is not subject to *rati-ic* knowledge of the piano through muscle memory and technical ability to execute so many notes in the right order and in time. Rather, the child's freedom to choose to act upon that which makes him happy is dependent upon the existence of something already present within himself. There is a specific orientation to piano playing as an activity that makes him happy *already within him*. He has an increased natural ability to experience this happiness through action in the physical world.

In this, happiness becomes a habit of goodness. The child requires less and less effort to be happy and has a corresponding increased level of personality. He has a decreased inhibition in his pursuit of happiness, culminating in experiential knowledge, beholding the whole activity as one integrated experience, known with the light of *intellectus*. Freedom, in this case, is "bestowed in the embryo" through the subject's natural inclinations at the moment of conception; it is then "developed through education and exercised, with discipline, through successive stages."[152]

This is the most appropriate way to speak of *vocation*: Each individual is drawn to and sees God in different, specific experiences of the physical realities in life. Each person pursues God through the different and personal calling in his heart. God Himself, then, behaves toward us according to the personalistic norm. He allows us to experience reality as subjects with our own subjective experiences. He is the author of this subjectivity within us, granting us personalities through the dictates of anamnesis, causing each actor happiness when he encounters God in different activities and perspectives.

The choice between conflicting goods is the task of the will; the *ability* to choose between goods is properly called freedom. Since that which inclines us to consider something as good is at the heart of personhood through the whispers of *anamnesis*, it is most appropriate to say that "freedom is at the heart of our existence. It is at the core of our experience and is the source of our willing and acting. It is who we are, at our most personal."[153] Each person is a unique subject to whom

152. Pinckaers, *The Sources of Christian Ethics*, 375.
153. Pinckaers, *The Sources of Christian Ethics*, 328.

God speaks directly in the recesses of the heart through a memory of the good. Hence, freedom emerges as inviolable within the individual.

Freedom also presents as accompanied by the responsibility to consistently choose that which aligns most closely with the whispers of their conscience. We move toward that which we determine to be good, trying to determine the best course of action in the face of conflicting goods. In the case of conflicting goods, the motivations and impulses to pursue one or another are seen as "conflicting interests" since we can distinguish between several goods we might otherwise be inclined to pursue.

Here, we finally have a look at the subjectivity of the person as it relates to the objectivity of the moral order. Humans can only encounter and cultivate a unique relationship with God through their subjective, corruptible bodily senses. The actor then chooses to pursue God in the specific way He reveals Himself to the person through *anamnesis*, causing the actor, in turn, to recollect or recognize God through the senses. This recognition comes from acting upon those specific goods manifesting themselves as legitimate desires.

What we have said correlates perfectly with our discussion on the personalistic norm in the previous chapter. The natural moral order itself—and indeed all of creation—in light of the personalistic norm, is far from a dull and impersonal data mine from which we choose what we will and extract information. On the contrary, the natural moral order actually "acquires personalistic attributes: the order of nature, since its framework accommodates personal entities as well as others, must possess such attributes."[154] Because God reveals Himself to the subjective person through the senses, Man constantly seeks God by pursuing the personal, legitimate desires of his heart.

The personalistic norm dictates that an individual's freedom, properly conceived of, must never be violated: Man must be permitted to seek God because he has the *obligation* to seek God; Man must be a good steward of creation because all of Creation is the vestigia of God by which God calls Man to Himself.

It is paramount, then, that societies arrange themselves in such a way that the individual freedom of the person is upheld and promoted. Persons of society must be free to choose excellence, always choosing that which brings them closer to happiness, according to the pursuit of the individual encounter with God, recognized because it has been previously written on their hearts. We shall return to those actions which promote or inhibit freedom presently.

---

154. John Paul II, *Love and Responsibility,* 27.

The Good and Freedom After Descartes

Classical thinkers behold the world as good: A thing is *good* inasmuch as it exists. The more a thing exists—the more actual it is, and is more itself—the more good it is. Viewing existence as good is made possible in this school of thought because of the fundamental premise and attitude toward knowledge: classical philosophy's *beholding* reality with a sense of *contemplative wonder*. Everything we have discussed thus far concerning the good stems from an epistemology driven by *dialectic*: using *ratio* to obtain an *intellectus* understanding of the whole of reality.

However, as the preceding chapters revealed, we in the twenty-first century have not inherited the classical epistemology as a societal norm. Rather, our world has been inundated and heavily formed by the Cartesian new epistemology. In inheriting its revolutionizing orientation toward knowledge, modern Man sees reality not as something to be encountered and contemplated, but rather as something to be seen through the lens of radical skepticism. Reality in this light is something to be conquered and overcome. The physical world is discounted as unintelligible; as a result, evil and good become mere opinions and perceptions. Moreover, freedom is no longer understood as an inherent attribute aimed toward the good; rather, it is considered a right that allows the actor to choose from a near-infinite array of possible motivations. To understand our own time better, it is necessary to examine the effects of Cartesian skepticism a little more closely.

Thought as the Good

The radical skepticism of Descartes:

> Distanced us from the philosophy of existence, and also from the traditional approaches of St. Thomas which lead to God who is 'autonomous existence'. . . By making subjective consciousness absolute, Descartes moves instead toward *pure consciousness of the Absolute*, which is pure thought. Such an absolute is not autonomous existence, but rather autonomous thought. Only that which corresponds to human thought makes sense. The objective truth of this thought is not

> as important as the fact that something exists in human consciousness . . . the consequence was that *man was supposed to live by his reason alone, as if God did not exist.* Not only was it necessary to leave God out of the objective knowledge of the world, since the existence of a Creator or of Providence was in no way helpful to science, it was also necessary to act as if God did not exist, as if God were not interested in the world.[155]

The change post-Descartes is a shift from *existence*—since we could not really know that anything existed except for ourselves—to what we could know: *thought.* Existence is no longer *good,* and Man is no longer most happy when he chooses according to his orientation toward fuller existence. Instead of the highest good understood as *existence from Whom all existence originates,* the highest good is now the thought from which all *thought* originates.

This shift claims that Man is oriented toward that which allows him to *think* more: He is, therefore, happiest when he is able to perceive more *context* within the world. Man's orientation, in this view, is toward what allows him to *infer* meaning upon experiences, to "*determine the meaning* of [his own] behavior."[156] There is no place for *anamnesis* in this worldview

---

155. John Paul II, *Crossing the Threshold of Hope*, ed. Vittorio Messori (New York, NY: Knopf, 2005), 45, Kindle.
156. John Paul II, *Veritatis Splendor*, para. 47.

because *anamnesis* only sees the world through one context: an encounter with God. God becomes a *threat* to autonomous thought since He imposes Himself upon Man's individual subjective experience. The need for God, therefore, dissipates into a frantic need to *expel* God from any consequential presence in the world. Man makes himself into a sort of anti-existence.

Cartesian Freedom

The foundational principle in classical philosophy's stance toward human action and freedom is that we all act toward the good—though sometimes we act on nothing more than what we perceive to be good. In this view, freedom is a choice between various goods. Man is more free when he is able to determine which good brings him truer happiness. The will is not *impartial* but is influenced toward choosing some goods over others.

A post-Cartesian world, however, asserts that freedom must include no such influence on the will. The main innovation of the will in this new outlook, which develops from placing the realm of reality solely within the mind and autonomous thought, is outlined by Pinckaers in his book *The Sources of Christian Ethics*. He describes the articulation of a monk named Ockham that the will can, in fact, "choose between contraries, and this power reside[s] in the will alone." Rather than reasoning what is best and acting upon it, Man *actually* possesses the power to choose "between what reason dictated and its contrary . . . [with a] radical indifference in the will regarding contraries."[157]

The will in this view is, in its purest, most free form, entirely ambivalent toward either good or evil. Man does not choose between paths toward happiness but can "choose or refuse happiness, either in particular matters . . . or in general . . . I could choose to preserve my life or to loathe my existence."[158] This assertion effectively holds that *any* inclination is artificial or, at worst, is an impediment to freedom. As a particularly poignant illustration, Ockham is explicitly claiming here that the basic first inclination of all beings we mentioned in Chapter II, i.e., to preserve my own existence, is thereby simply a matter of the will. In his mind, it is not an inclination at all—there are no natural inclinations.

We were able to spend a considerable amount of time treating the good and the inclination toward it featured in classical philosophy. By contrast, we find ourselves quickly arriving at the chaotic conclusion of post-Cartesian freedom almost as soon as it begins. The will, being equally indifferent toward every choice, is *weakened* and freedom *violated* by any sort of inclination that does not originate within the subject himself. Influences on a person's will become "the most insidious threat to freedom and the morality of

---

157. Pinckaers, *The Sources of Christian Ethics*, 332.
158. Pinckaers, *The Sources of Christian Ethics*, 333.

actions"[159] because they infringe upon the foundational indifference to any choice. *Anamnesis*, at the very core of personhood, "appears here not as a window through which one can see outward to that common truth that founds and sustains us all,"[160] but as a pesky influence that must be escaped if we are to be free.

The irony in this severance from reality is seen when one considers the requirements this radical freedom of indifference imposes upon the subject. Because any kind of influence must be discounted as unduly inclining the will and, therefore, is a violation of freedom, Man is forced to also be *free from himself.* The experiences of Man cannot be allowed to have consequences in his own life: Every single action must be "held fixed in the instant of choice and separated from all the actions preceding or following it . . . we [can] not allow our past actions to determine the action of the present moment, nor [can] the latter have any bearing upon what we might do in the future."[161]

In the entirely isolating ramification of this philosophy, Man is challenged to avoid his experience, the physical world, and the inner voice within himself. The physical world, through which we encounter everything that exists, is deemed not only *unintelligible* but *dangerous to personal dignity and freedom.* Man has essentially become trapped and enslaved in every

---

159. Pinckaers, *The Sources of Christian Ethics*, 333.
160. Ratzinger, "Erroneous Conscience."
161. Pinckaers, *The Sources of Christian Ethics*, 337.

particular instant, paradoxically resulting in less possible freedom or happiness than is possible even for those born into physical slavery. Let us look at the slavery of the fallen angels to illustrate.

The experience of the angels is largely beyond the scope of our discussions. This being said, considering how freedom is experienced by the fallen angels lends itself as a perfect example of the paradoxical lack of freedom that freedom as *license* to choose evil provides.

The fallen angels experience a lack of freedom in an intense and unadulterated way. Because "each angel understands himself by his form . . . [and] it is through [the form of his own species] that he understands himself . . . an angel's knowledge of himself is incapable of error, and his knowledge of himself is perfect."[162] Because of our discussion on the image of God, we know that angels, too, partake in that divine image. As such, when an angel understands himself, he sees "God's image impressed on the very nature of the angel in his essence, so the angel knows God inasmuch as he is in the image of God."[163]

The fallen angels "have chosen to hate God and His Holy Will," believing pride and nonservice to bring more happiness than serving God. However, even fallen angels retain the divine image. In their understanding of themselves, they still recognize that image. As

---

162. Ripperger, *Dominion*, 8.
163. Ripperger, *Dominion*, 8.

such, "when they see that in their nature, they experience a self-loathing and hatred."[164] Far from becoming happy in their ability to choose, the angels are plagued with misery and a "tremendous affliction."[165]

Completely autonomous freedom—*autonomy* in this sense meaning free from any sort of outside influence—inverts the very powers of the soul and makes the cognitive subject to the appetitive. In the isolated, uninfluenced search for specific and personal happiness, Man confuses what *will* make him happy with the movements of his passions. He desires to pursue only that which he is able to choose for himself, lusting after the power to create his own good—the power which belongs to God alone.

The word *lust* is most appropriate here, considering *anamnesis* is a *loving* beckoning that God places in Man. When someone desires that which ought to be given and received between persons in love out of rather a desire for possession and domination—in this case, to *use* reality for one's own benefits—the only proper word is *lust*.

Speaking of revolution against the dictates of *anamnesis* opens our discussion to clearly illustrate the movements within the soul when the actor lives this way. Lust is a movement of the lower powers that overcome the higher powers in matters of personhood and love. It hinders the higher powers and makes them

164. Ripperger, *Dominion*, 8.
165. Ripperger, *Dominion*, 8.

"disordered in their acts . . . Consequently the higher powers, namely the reason and the will, are most grievously disordered by lust."[166]

In this revolution within the soul, Aquinas says the intellect suffers four blindnesses: a distortion of simple understanding (*blindness of the mind*), a failure to develop correct counsel on proper action to take for the sake of the end (*rashness*), improper judgment on what is to be done (*thoughtlessness*), and a lessening of the command of reason in relation to what is to be done, i.e., the reason does not hold sufficient power to dictate actions (*inconstancy*). All this to say, sin makes one stupid.

Perhaps the easiest place to see these disastrous results is in the effects pornography has on individuals. There is a push to "normalize" pornography as if it were a harmless, natural activity. The data, however, illustrates a different story. Far from being a commonplace, normal, or healthy occurrence, studies state that pornography use is "most frequently done out of boredom."[167] Though other reasons for pornography use are listed, boredom is usually listed first among the common motives. What is more, according to this study published only recently, pornography use is far from

166. Aquinas, *Summa Theologiae,* q. 153.

167. Haseeb Mehmood Qadri, et al., "Physiological, Psychosocial and Substance Abuse Effects of Pornography Addiction: A Narrative Review," *Cureus*, January 12, 2023, accessed September 19, 2024, https://www.ncbi.nlm.nih.gov/pmc/articles/PMC9922938/.

harmless. In fact, "in all facets of users' lives, negative consequences were seen. [Its widespread use] has very injurious effects on societies and individuals."[168] The specifically identified negative effects? Though only about half of the studies list negative *physical* effects (ED, addiction, etc.), nearly all studies list negative psychological effects:

> Low mood, depression, decreased self-esteem, decreased appetite, etc. The emotional effects of porn include: getting irritable when disturbed while watching porn, not being able to quit it even for a day, and watching women undress in real life to fulfill their desires. The social effects of porn include social awkwardness, inability to concentrate at work, decreased family interaction, and increased cybercrimes such as cyberstalking and pedophilia.[169]

Though the first of the four blindnesses (*decreased simple understanding*) is an *intuited* consequence of the other negative effects, we can see listed clearly the remaining three. We see *rashness* in the suggested irritability and the inability to quit among porn users. Awkwardness, cybercrimes, and general creepiness are parallels to *thoughtlessness*. And finally, depression,

---

168. Qadri, et al., "Effects of Pornography Addiction."
169. Qadri, et al., "Effects of Pornography Addiction."

inability to concentrate, and decreased familial interaction are all similar to *inconstancy*.

If we accept our premise that what and how we encounter the world further informs how we understand the world (the senses precede reason in the order of origination), then we can easily intuit that all these negative effects inform the intellect in an erroneous way. Therefore, we even see that there is a distorted capacity for simple understanding, making all four blindnesses present in our current example.

Whereas in sin (always a form of lust), the intellect suffers four blindnesses, the will, on the other hand, suffers only one attack, but with complex results. A will in the clutches of lust suffers an inordinate desire for pleasure. This intense desire results in both excessive love of self and hatred of God, Who is perceived to forbid the pursuit of pleasure. In addition to the love of self, the will experiences "'love of this world,' whose pleasures a man desires to enjoy, while on the other hand, there is 'despair of a future world,' because through being held back by carnal pleasures he cares not to obtain spiritual pleasures, since they are distasteful to him."[170] Thus, the inversion of freedom becomes complete: Love of God becomes love of self, and freedom as choosing God is discarded for the notion that choosing the self is an option in true freedom.

The effects of man's search for *himself* as opposed to searching for God result in the complete

170. Aquinas, *Summa Theologiae,* q. 153.

unintelligibility of reality. The world is recreated into a nightmarish experience, resulting in a foundational fear of the reality now only known through the context and meaning Man himself bestows upon it.

John Paul II writes about the fear Man experiences in such a reality in his encyclical *Redemptor Hominis.* Here, he claims that "the man of today seems ever to be under threat from what he produces, that is to say from the result of the work of his hands and, even more so, of the work of his intellect and the tendencies of his will."[171] In his desire to *be* God, Man is constantly aware of his own subverting the moral order. He lives in fear that his own creation will do to him what he himself tries to do to God.

The sentiment surrounding Man's inherent fear of his own creations is made explicit in many of the mainstream pop culture, especially in movies portraying technological advances. In such media, technology begins as a life-enhancing creation of Man. Many times, either through science reaching too far or the inevitability of autonomous thought, the tech grows and runs amok. No longer an enhancer, Man's creation changes into "the means and instrument for an unimaginable self-destruction, compared with which all the cataclysms and catastrophes of history known to us seem to fade away."[172] Man's freedom becomes threatened

---

171. John Paul II, *Redemptor Hominis* (Vatican City: Vatican Press, 1979), paragraph 15.
172. John Paul II, *Redemptor Hominis*, para. 15.

by machines that have become self-aware and, therefore, able to inflict their own will upon humans as if in retaliation for Man imposing *his* will on them.

Through freedom of indifference, Man is not only isolated *within* himself through the creation of his own reality but is also *tortured and petrified with fear*. We must conclude our discussion of perceivable reality as now becoming an insidious threat to the self, as opposed to something to be encountered. Instead, let us turn our eyes forward. We must discuss a return to true freedom.

A Return to Freedom

The rejection of true freedom, articulated by Ockham and orchestrated before him by the new epistemology of Descartes, has become widespread and all-encompassing, a foundational understanding held by nearly all. We who would return to a classical understanding of freedom and happiness are left, in a sense, at a disadvantage with a seemingly impossible task ahead of us. The evidence of this challenge is apparent as a result of our claims throughout this discussion.

We ourselves are not immune to the societal embrace of the freedom of indifference. Subconsciously, we too embody and sometimes act as though freedom is absolute autonomy and develop within ourselves a nefariously disguised intellectual cowardice in relating to our neighbor. Only by confronting the pervasive notion of freedom, by calling its name, can we hope to free ourselves from our inherited bondage.

The Impossible Chasm

If we are to believe that our experiences *matter,* that we can know only by what we experience through the senses, then we are forced to realize that we ourselves have been foundationally influenced by the age-long domain of freedom of indifference. It is the only freedom we have encountered or have been encouraged to pursue in our societal environments. We find ourselves in a position where we "no longer realize the nature of the catastrophe which [we have] suffered"[173] in losing classical freedom. Words such as *freedom* and *good* are colloquially so far removed from their authentic meanings that the fact that we may "be being betrayed by the very language [we] use is not a thought available to [us]."[174]

People trapped in a modern world, attempting a return to something they do not remember, often memorize and articulate the isolated sayings and writings of prior philosophers. Well-meaning individuals turn to these works and read them as best as they are able: individually, but without context or view of the whole—fragments of what has come before. These fragments "conform to certain canons of consistency

173. MacIntyre, *After Virtue,* 3.
174. MacIntyre, *After Virtue*, 4.

and coherence," and as a result, these people do not realize that "those contexts which would be needed to make sense of what they are doing have been lost"[175]

Many who proclaim a return to exercising a freedom that reflects God's presence in our lives still largely cannot conceive of an alternative reality to the one that claims, "Man, as a rational being, not only can but actually *must freely determine the meaning* of his behavior." Modern attempts to return to freedom, rather than viewing freedom as preserved by the moral order, can often do no better than to *concede* freedom to God's higher power, asserting in Christian faith that "this process of 'determining the meaning' would obviously have to take into account the many limitations of the human being . . . [and] would have to respect the fundamental commandment of love of God and neighbor."[176] Finally, though we feel the call within our hearts that God is our ultimate happiness, we maintain that the basic precept of freedom requires us to hold our neighbor in such autonomy that we must still "above all and even exclusively respect . . . his freedom to make his own decisions."[177]

This well-intentioned attempt to return to a pseudo-classical freedom is doomed from the start. Attempts at articulating a binding moral order are simply incompatible with the belief that freedom grants the ability to

175. MacIntyre, *After Virtue*, 1.
176. John Paul II, *Veritatis Splendor*, para. 47.
177. John Paul II, *Veritatis Splendor*, para. 47.

choose evil. *Anamnesis* has no place or benefit in such systems, for its presence would mean that God Himself violates Man's free will. Instead of being a foundational beckoning toward God, which exhorts even those who have never heard the Gospel to earnestly do good and avoid sin, *anamnesis* must be simply absent in Man from the beginning. The only moral choice available to Man is to *ignore* the lower instincts of his nature. The will must brace itself for false heroism, holding with white knuckles to an imposed morality and regarding all lower inclinations as traitors to a happiness Man is convicted of but feels can only be realized in some abstract future. Man must choose "happiness," even though his desires seem to beckon him contrary.

The modern Man, entrapped in a world of freedom of indifference, envies those people who appear allowed by God to be "unbelievers in good conscience. For if their eyes were opened and they became believers, they would not be capable, in this world of ours, of bearing the burden of faith with all its moral obligations. But as it is, since they can go another way in good conscience, they can still reach salvation."[178] This is a mentality that encourages intellectual cowardice. Feigning respect for personal freedom, it passes itself as kindness, claiming it is an act of charity to leave others in moral ignorance. The thought goes: Once a person is made aware of the moral order, they are

---

178. Ratzinger, "Erroneous Conscience."

burdened to follow the rules of a morality they were heretofore free from.

The underlying sentiment that envies those people who seem to have been given a license to do ill with no personal responsibility is encapsulated by the story of the Grand Inquisitor. This fictional malcontent claims that God has endowed man with "some promise of freedom which men in their simplicity and their natural unruliness cannot even understand, which they fear and dread—since nothing has ever been more insupportable for a man and a human society than freedom!"[179] And indeed, according to our discussion on freedom of indifference, freedom is unbearable in light of our lower passions!

As long as such grave misunderstandings are the foundation of a countermovement against modernity, any coherent attempt at a revival of happiness understood as an orientation toward God is bound to fail. The first premise to return to for those who would understand freedom is a recognition of a reality outside of ourselves, which can be perceived *as it is* and does not depend on our own imposition of meaning onto reality. Recognition of a reality that influences us, along with admitting an already existing *anamnesis* within

179. Dostoyevsky, "The Grand Inquisitor."
Blavatsky translates this as offering a "vague and undefined promise of freedom, which men, dull and unruly as they are by nature, are unable so much as to understand, which they avoid and fear?—for never was there anything more unbearable to the human race than personal freedom!"

ourselves, provides the much-needed return from the nightmarish abyss Man has condemned himself to.

Return to Freedom

In the return to classical epistemology pioneered by Pope John Paul II, our subjective experience of reality through the senses—and therefore the acts of the will—influences and shapes the person himself. We are not left unaffected by our own choices: We are either drawn toward the good (an encounter with God) or are inclined further away from Him as a result of the nature, intent, and objective morality of our actions. In this, as we have seen, freedom is not the ability to choose any number of options, but rather is the ability to see and choose the good. The difference here is really between being enslaved to chasing transitive goods or having the freedom to *be* happy.

One of the most accessible experiences of the slavery/freedom dichotomy as it plays out within the interior of the individual, illustrating the consequence of an outside reality upon ourselves, is the common struggle to quit smoking. After having smoked for countless years, an individual who decides to quit is afflicted both by the habitual *act* of smoking and the chemical dependence on nicotine. Physical suffering, headaches, irritability, and other characteristics mark the struggles surrounding the attempt to quit. As a result, many cave and continue with the habit. In a word, these individuals are *not free* to quit smoking in order to enjoy the health and financial benefits of a smoke-free life. They remain shackled to the habit. It is not the choice to smoke that makes one free; it is both the ability to determine when you *want* to stop and the ability to actually choose to stop that makes one free.

Admitting that there *is,* in fact, an outside reality external to ourselves that affects us allows us to admit that there is something intrinsic to Man that orients him in one way or another. Moreover, it paves the way to consider outside influences on my will as not bad *per se*—not an automatic violation of my freedom. Once more, we can reject the notion that demands Man be suspended in abstract nothingness, with an infinite number of choices to choose from. We can admit that within the heart of each person is some inclination that allows him to *recognize* that when something makes him happy, it is an encounter and an opportunity to see an aspect of God revealed through that experience. In this world, Man is not condemned—nor indeed able—to blindly search for happiness among so many objects around him, choosing each in turn in an attempt to experience them as an experiment on the path to self-knowledge. In short, admitting an external reality and the *benefit* of environmental influence begins the revolution, which returns to anamnesis as a foundational orientation toward an encounter with God through specific physical encounters with Him in the vestigia of the world. It is the very principle of uniqueness in each person, wherein every person in the recesses of his heart "recognize[s God] . . . [and] irresistibly flock to Him, they surround Him, they form about Him, follow Him."[180]

Anamnesis as a good allows us to remember that freedom, seen as an absolute, leads Man toward the complete erasure of the subjective individual himself:

> A freedom which claims to be absolute ends up treating the human body as a raw datum, devoid of any meaning and moral values until freedom has shaped it in accordance with its design. Consequently, human nature and the body appear as *presuppositions or preambles,* materially *necessary* for freedom to make its choice, yet extrinsic to the person, the subject and the human act.[181]

Remembering that happiness is not a personal invention, that our soul longs to ascend, is the only path that returns Man to freedom.

---

180. Dostoyevsky, "The Grand Inquisitor."

181. John Paul II, *Veritatis Splendor*, para. 48.

Original Sin and the Loss of Conscience

Freedom in light of *anamnesis* is a hearkening of the heart. It is a quiet in the soul which allows Man to see and hear the specific beckoning God instills in each person to choose Him as the Chief Source of happiness, however He presents Himself in the physical world. Freedom is thus tied to a restlessness of the will, desiring goods only insofar as they lead to God.

We have already introduced verbiage denoting moral weight to the dictates of happiness as a pursuit of the good, suggesting that pursuing what fails to bring happiness is the absence of good we call *sin.* The language of sin, however, might appear somewhat problematic and requires examination.

The connotation of sin is to assign culpability, moral responsibility, and guilt to a person as a judgment upon their actions. The problem arises when we are reminded that freedom is not acting with no influence at all, but that:

> No one may act against his convictions, as St. Paul had already said (Romans l4:23). But this fact . . . does not signify a canonization of subjectivity. It is never wrong to follow the convictions one has arrived at—in fact, one must do so. But it can very well be wrong to have come to such askew convictions in the first place, by having stifled the protest of the anamnesis of being."[182]

How, then, are we to *trust* that *anamnesis* is *truly* directing us toward true happiness?

This question introduces a secondary problem: What are we to make then of the supposed justice of original sin? It is an inherited action that we do not bear direct responsibility for. Nonetheless, the effects of original sin clearly have an influence on our experience of anamnesis. Our premise is that *anamnesis* is a fundamental orientation toward the good, but faith informs us that we are inclined toward sin as an effect of Adam's sin. Has our entire discussion on *anamnesis* thus been rendered null?

---

182. Ratzinger, "Systematic Consequences."

Opinions on what is good or permissible change over time. Someone who previously lived a righteous life can easily begin a life of revelry, as if now deaf to the moral voice he once heeded. As a consequence of our actions (or through the effects of original sin), is it possible to lose the ability to hear the dictates of *anamnesis* entirely? Can we be erroneously drawn toward that which is *not* good so that we, like the Pharisee, no "longer know that [we] too [have] guilt[?] [We have] a completely clear conscience,"[183] and are thereby free to do as we please?

Finally, we have gone to such pains to show that *anamnesis* is *the* defining point of personhood and the source that demands dignity and respect for life. We must ask if those who have lost the voice of *anamnesis* are, therefore, considered *less than people.* Have they somehow lost their own personhood and, therefore, any right or obligation to dignity and freedom? We will examine the specific ramifications of sin at this time.

Original Sin

The most appropriate way to speak of freedom is specifically in the context of sin. Freedom is the ability to avoid and resist the slavelike urges of fallen human nature, to sell what we have and follow Christ. This slave language as relates to sin is consistent throughout the Scriptures, especially in the writings of Paul, where he

183. Ratzinger, "Erroneous Conscience."

says, "What I do, I do not understand. For I do not do what I want, but I do what I hate."[184]

Belief in personal power to define the good effectively causes us to wrest our own freedom from ourselves. Imposing our will upon reality in a futile attempt to "do what we want" (freedom *from* restraint) dooms us to the dictates of our passions, rendering us unable to flourish and navigate reality (freedom *for* the good).

The apparent problem in this can now be raised: Is not one of the prime results of original sin that we experience heightened passions, weakened will, and a darkened intellect so that we can no longer readily know the good, want the good, and orient our passions toward the good? Are we not born already with the stain of someone else's sin on our hearts? Barring the Immaculate Conception, there is no part of creation that has not been touched by this sin, no conscience that is immune from a clouded view of the good. It would seem that we are left in a state where we can *use* the word *sin* but are so fundamentally separated from understanding of the good, unadulterated by original sin, that we have lost the sense of what sin is.

Sin, in its "original form" as laid out in the Genesis narrative and upheld throughout the Old Testament, "is understood as 'disobedience,' and this means simply and directly transgression of a prohibition laid down

184. Romans 7:15.

by God."[185] The original sin of Adam was directly, of course, eating the fruit of the tree. In this, our own individual sins are not unlike his original sin, inasmuch as we choose what *we* decide or determine is good as opposed to what is *actually* good. We, too, commit the sin of *disobedience,* which itself "means precisely going beyond [the limits set by God], which remain impassable to the will and the freedom of man as a created being."[186]

Though we can see some parallels between our own sins and that first sin of Adam, the culpability and participation in original sin is Adam's alone. We do not partake in the responsibility for actions that we do not commit. The *effects* of original sin, however, are another story entirely. The internal logic of this statement is evident from our discussion and emphasis thus far on the inescapable effects of the physical world outside of ourselves.

Through the sin of Adam, all of creation fell. As a result of this fall, we inherit a darkened intellect, weakened will, and heightened passions. Original sin is not some transgression that we ourselves have specific responsibility for; rather, "original sin denotes the privation of original justice, and besides this, the inordinate disposition of the parts of the soul. Consequently, it is not a pure privation, but a corrupt habit."[187] Original

---

185. John Paul II, *Dominum et Vivificantem*, para. 36.
186. John Paul II, *Dominum et Vivificantem*, para. 36.
187. Aquinas, *Summa Theologiae,* q. 82, art. 1.

sin is a preexisting *habit*, a privation already within our soul because of the fall of the original man, communicated to us by virtue of being born *into* sin.

Our own sins are not severed as to have no relation to the sin of Adam, however. Just as Adam disobeyed God in that first sin and turned away from Him, so too our own "disobedience always means a turning away from God, and in a certain sense, the closing up of human freedom in his regard. It also means a certain opening of this freedom—of the human mind and will—to the one who is the 'father of lies.'"[188] Not only do our *sins*—actions of "conscious choice" in disobedience to God—"involve a certain consent to the motivation which was contained in the first temptation to sin and which is unceasingly renewed during the whole history of man on earth,"[189] we also thereby contribute to the collective and hereditary effects of sin within the world. Our own sins reaffirm and participate in the *motivation* for sin originating from Adam, but our mere existence does not imply active participation in his sin. This much to say: Though we are not exempt from the effects of sin, existence itself is not sin.

A theological discussion of the Holy Spirit is beyond the scope of our discussions here. This being said, a brief mention of His workings in the world—especially as it relates to *anamnesis*—seems appropriate at this point. The Holy Spirit works within the

188. John Paul II, *Dominum et Vivificantem*, para. 37.
189. John Paul II, *Dominum et Vivificantem*, para. 37.

individual's *anamnesis,* enabling him to recognize sin for what it is: choosing a lesser or inappropriate good as if it were the highest good. This internal conviction concerning the nature of sin is necessary for individuals to acknowledge it; therefore, the Holy Spirit is necessary for a rejection of sin.

Man always retains an orientation to follow the natural law as written upon his heart, in spite of the effects of original sin. He can, to a greater or lesser degree, recognize and act upon the good as he cooperates with this law or rejects it. A properly formed conscience, utilizing the dictates of reason and cooperating with the moving of the Holy Spirit, equips the individual (who in turn builds society) to see sin for what it is. This is the final telos of *anamnesis* and the prerequisite for true freedom: "to call good and evil by their proper name."[190]

The Name of Sin and Where Sin Lies

Understanding original sin is foundational for regarding evil as an absurdity of nonexistence, requiring a *response* rather than *understanding* evil itself. Christ came and paid the debt of Man. Through His response as crucified Messiah, He reintroduced the Holy Spirit into the world, who convinces the world of sin.

The Holy Spirit restores freedom and a new sense of identity into the hearts of Men. This is one way in

190. John Paul II, *Dominum et Vivificantem*, para. 37.

which we might advantageously reflect on the concept of being *"born again,"* for it is quite literally true that our personhood is changed and given new life through the working of the Holy Spirit at the foundational levels of our hearts. We must now examine what exactly this sin is that the Holy Spirit convinces Man of and how He does so.

The word *sin* has a connotation of culpability, of responsibility, and of intent, and rightly so. We have already determined that the biblical understanding of *sin* is one of *disobedience* or turning away from God. To turn away from God, practically speaking, does not require intention: *Anamnesis* orients us always *toward* an encounter with God, though this does not mean that we will find Him where we look. We can turn toward what we *think* will make us happy, but be mistaken. However, *culpability* for turning away from God is required for us to regard it as *disobedience,* and culpability does require intent.

Understanding the will as searching and acting upon happiness reveals the specific twisting of a good, which results in sin. Happiness at the misfortunes of my enemies is not *happiness that my enemy is suffering misfortune,* but rather happiness in what I might perceive to be justice. In my search for justice, I stumble upon anger or uncharity—as in harboring happiness at the misfortunes of my enemy. The good desired is still justice; only in my inability to recognize it do I miss justice and instead harbor a vengeful uncharity.

How can I be sure that my own actions and intentions are not sinful and are aimed at God Himself? Are we to assume that whoever does not believe in God in an explicit way is in a constant state of perpetual sin? We can answer these questions by briefly looking at individual cooperation with the Holy Spirit as He works to convince Man of his own sin.

Cooperating with the Holy Spirit means only and faithfully acting upon what we perceive as good in the world to develop the habit of freely choosing the good. Only by doing the good are we able to *see* the greatest good. By cooperating in this way, we *properly form our conscience.* Continually choosing the good develops our ability to recognize the voice of the Holy Spirit in our own hearts. When we are endowed with a properly formed conscience, and such a habit is formed, we find ourselves like the child playing the piano: able to improvise and trust our own talent. In our freedom, we enjoy a recognition of what is really good, stemming from within us in a unique and incommunicable way.

This is not to say that we cannot change, silence, or ignore the whispers of the Holy Spirit to such a great extent that we lose recognition of our own actions as being aimed *away* from what brings true happiness. On the contrary, this is, in fact, very possible and is what Christ would call the *unforgivable sin.* The *unforgivable sin* is the sin never repented of, precisely because *the sense of sin in the subject has been lost due to a constant, repeated, and intentional silencing—and therefore expulsion—of God's welcome in the recesses of the heart.* At this stage, the subject not only "rejects the 'convincing concerning sin' which comes from the Holy Spirit and which has the power to save," but he also "rejects the 'coming' of the Counselor—that 'coming' which was accomplished in the Paschal Mystery, in union with the redemptive power of Christ's blood: the Blood which 'purifies the conscience from dead works.'"[191] In his rejection of the Holy Spirit, the actor redefines the good in an invincible way to his own mind. He refuses to acknowledge his own need for forgiveness because he rejects the unlooked-for mercy of God in its entirety from the Cross to his own life.

This, then, is the image of a Man who deems himself capable of happiness and goodness left to his own devices: He is lost without his own sense of identity in a perpetually spiraling nightmare of his own creation, harboring animosity and contempt at the suggestion that he needs any outside intervention in his life. This lost soul no "longer knows that he too has guilt. He has a completely clear conscience. But this silence of conscience makes him impenetrable to God and men"[192] to such an extent that he is entirely encapsulated in his own isolation.

Losing the capability to *hear anamnesis* does not mean that the voice of *anamnesis* is not present, however. Such a Man is still a *person* because that unique

---

191. John Paul II, *Dominum et Vivificantem*, para. 46.
192. Ratzinger, "Erroneous Conscience."

recognition of what makes him happy still *exists.* Nevertheless, his inability to *recognize* what brings him happiness makes his unique experience of the world torturous, rendering him unintelligible and unrecognizable as the person he truly is. His manifestations and communications of himself to others become so distorted from reality that they are entirely false, lacking context, and absurd in themselves. For the sake of his *anamnesis* and the image of God on his soul, even he must not be made an object of use. The personalistic norm still applies. However, we would be wise not to interact to a great extent or seek a friendship with such a Man.

Where Sin Lies

Seeking selfish happiness, acting on the world with a conquering, possessive intent rather than through the receptive contemplation of the vestigia, encouraging encounter, is to violate the personalistic norm as applied to God. To see something as merely an object for our own gratification is to ignore what God is speaking to us at that moment. It is, in a sense, to use *Him* as an object for use, inasmuch as the object in question is His way of communicating with us. Every action we choose that violates this principle of the personalistic norm affects us since we are shaped by our actions. Therefore, it is not the *action itself* but rather the choice and the intent behind the action wherein the sin lies.

Sin, we remember, is to be understood as disobedience that is accompanied by culpability, not just any action that results in a negative impact upon our *anamnesis*. We can choose something, thinking it to be a good, but be mistaken. An easy example in which to see this play out is the relative state of undress in which the "uncontacted tribes" in tropical climates live. Do these tribes sin against the requirements of chastity or modesty in their nakedness? We shall use their cultural habits, which seem to sanction an act denounced as morally wrong elsewhere in the world, to better understand where sin lies.

Pope John Paul II comments on the relative state of undress experienced in less developed cultures in his book *Love and Responsibility*. Here, he writes that:

> [I]n tropical conditions primitive peoples live in partial or total nakedness. Many details in their way of life indicate that nakedness cannot be simply and unambiguously identified with shamelessness. On the contrary . . . the concealment of parts of the body previously exposed is a manifestation of shamelessness. We doubtless see here the effect of habit, of a collective custom . . . Sexual modesty cannot then in any simple way be identified with the use of clothing, nor shamelessness with the absence of clothing and total or partial nakedness.[193]

---

193. John Paul II, *Love and Responsibility*, 175–176.

At face value, it would seem that morality really does depend on the constructs of the society in which one finds oneself. Anything could be acceptable as long as everyone within the society finds themselves on the same page and consents to the actions of others. Pope John Paul II himself acknowledged that the nakedness of these tribes is almost certainly a cultural habit. Nonetheless, we would not be correct to conclude that morality is a relative construct, subject to the collective conscience of any society. There somehow remains an objective morality.

The arguments for a totally subjective view of morality and the social construct of virtue exist on a plane of intersection between objective morality, subjective actions, and the dictates of conscience. To say there is an objective morality does not negate the obligation to follow the dictates of conscience, nor does it deny the subjective experience of reality. Likewise, to say that I am blameless for my sin because my conscience, formed in good faith and to the best of my ability, instructed me to act thusly (despite morality determining that to be an objectively objectionable action) does not, therefore, disprove the existence of objective morality or that I am still bound by its dictates despite my ignorance. Duty to morality, culpability, and subjectivity coexist within the intellect and the will of the human person.

Recentering around the example we have at hand: What does this mean for the objectivity of modest dress? The objective morality, binding upon all peoples of all times in all places, is to regard the other person not as an object of use but as a subject, independent and free to be encountered and loved. The subjective actions of societies, as they attempt to live up to this responsibility, differ according to custom and climate. Thus, it is possible that the naked man within the Amazon finds no shame in beholding the nakedness of women. To understand this situation, we must not so much consider the primitive tribe's *lack of shame,* but the relative *inappropriateness* that shame in their attire would present.

Shame is the appropriate interior response in the face of something intrinsically private that has been made public. Objectively, it is not the human body that is the private thing that must not be made public. Rather, it is the relative dangers of those bodies to elicit an attitude of use in the eyes of the beholder that is the private thing made public. In this context, we can consider it to be at times that it is the actual "concealment of those parts of the body which distinguish male and female [that the objectification of the person is perceived]. We find that dress may serve not only to conceal but in one way or another to draw attention to these parts of the body,"[194] drawing undue attention to the body as *objects with function* as opposed to a *manifestation of the person.* We can see, then, that in accord with the dictates of *anamnesis* in a unique way to

194. John Paul II, *Love and Responsibility*, 176.

different peoples, to some level, there is, in fact, an element of subjectivity in the specifics of what constitutes modesty in dress. This principle is easily extended into other areas or actions as well.

Once we get to speaking of objectivity in what constitutes modest dress, we run into the issue of specifics. It would be hard to create such a standard of modesty in dress. Modesty is an attempt at both presenting myself as a subject that must not be used and at preventing others from seeing me as an object for use. *Objectivity of truth* means that what is true must, therefore, be true for every person at all times in all places. But what would be the objective standard that allows me to present myself as a subject and is yet aimed at the subjectivity of others, discouraging both unintentional and malicious attitudes of use? Exactly what are the objective limits of dress? How low exactly does a skirt have to be? How long do a man's shirtsleeves have to be? How hot does it have to get to weigh the relative danger of modesty versus heatstroke? These and many other logistical impossibilities present themselves as barriers to determining a baseline standard for modesty in clothing outside of an *honest adherence to the dictates of a conscience properly formed and executed in true freedom.*

We can now apply our discussion on modest dress directly to the previously discussed tribes. If a culture sees female breasts, for example, as providing nourishment for children and not as sexually arousing, bare-breasted women are objectively not being shameless. She is not exposing anything publicly that is *intrinsically* private. Conversely, men who behold a woman so dressed would be right to shamelessly behold that woman. Thus, the level of modesty in dress goes two ways: The dresser must dress with regard to shame, and the beholder must behold in a manner that maintains a sense of shame.

Sexual modesty lies primarily within the will of the human person, not isolated within the individual actions themselves. Likewise, all sin lies primarily within the *will* of the individual subject and not in actions themselves. This is not to say that the actions of the person are not fruits and consequences of the will; actions are an integral part of true freedom and, therefore, also, to a certain extent, of sin.

We are forced to remember that our actions form us. Even if we are not culpable for the sin of our actions, we still find ourselves changed and oriented toward different things by those actions. In a somewhat hard-to-believe circumstance, if I am honestly clear in my conscience that overindulging in alcohol in one particular instance is not evil,[195] I might be free from the culpability of that sin. However, the effects of alcohol will still be a consequence of my action. As a result of this

---

195. In the name of "overindulgence," we see in this example what constitutes at least a *vincible* ignorance of the objective morality (thus creating the circumstances inhibiting belief).

action, in the future, I will still be more *inclined* toward a greater amount of alcohol. This is why we must at all times form our conscience in accord with objective morality and conduct ourselves in a manner that attests to our dignity and the dignity of others. Only then can we love and be loved in mutual self-gift and dignity.

We are now able to identify both the *name* of sin and *where* sin lies. *Sin* is a turning away from God, a disobedience to the foundational premise of the natural order that a person must never be merely an object of use. Though there are objective actions that do, *of their nature*, result in a person being made an object of use and are, therefore, *morally objectionable at all times to all people*, the individual culpability of participating in these actions can be mitigated by an invincible ignorance. You can still *do* evil from a place of ignorance; you cannot *disobey* a command you have authentically never received.

We can also see that not every action, which we might otherwise consider to *be* a sin, actually is, once the particular actor and the circumstances are judged. This is what is meant by the exhortation not to judge so that we might not be judged: that we not try to interpret a subject's honest attempt to respond to God's calling upon his heart. We must be committed to freedom in the proper sense of the word, allowing individuals to pursue God according to the movements He makes within their souls. Societies must be diligent in preserving this freedom as a basic human right, without which they are not able to be *truly* themselves. In our dealings with other people, we must always embody the precept that "only respect for life can be the foundation and guarantee of the most precious and essential goods of society."[196]

196. John Paul II, *Evangelium Vitae* (Vatican City: Vatican Press, 1995), paragraph 101.

Ability versus Imperative

Before we conclude our discussion on freedom and the will, we must recap something that has been lingering in the shadows of our argument—alluded to, articulated again and again, but only implicitly. We must touch upon the question of whether *ability* designates *right*. Put differently, if I have the *ability* to pursue something, does it mean that I have the *right* to do so? Just because I am capable, does it mean that I should, or do "ought" statements even lend themselves to the concept of freedom as it relates to ability? The answer to this question cannot be overstated: Capacity does *not* denote right, nor does it denote imperative. What is more, preserving the *capacity to choose the wrong* is never a responsibility of the community as a correlation to preserving the capacity to choose the good.

Evil and vice are *absences* of good. They do not have any bearing or dignity in themselves since they do not *exist*. Only the good *exists*, and only what is good preserves happiness, develops personhood, and encouraging encounter. Remembering that we are bound by the personalistic norm, and under that norm, we must preserve anything that benefits and upholds the dignity of the person; it follows that we are *not* required to preserve people's ability to choose evil. In fact, since society has a responsibility to preserve and promote freedom, the apparent imperative is to create an environment wherein individuals can develop their "ability to perform actions of real excellence by removing dangerous excesses, which can proliferate in the human person like weeds stifling good grain, by guarding [them] against unhealthy error that could turn [them] aside and jeopardize [their] interior freedom."[197]

It is an act of upholding the dignity of the person to allow him to become *more* able to *be*. Conversely, it is a violation of the personalistic norm to allow someone to devolve *away* from personhood. It is allowing a person to *use himself*, and thereby too to *use God*. In this, society becomes a teacher, and we become the guardians of our neighbors in the encouragement and formulation of a society bent on preserving the human conscience, allowing for the true following of anamnesis—but not to the extent of allowing evil as if preserving evil as a choice was integral to freedom.

---

197. Pinckaers, *The Sources of Christian Ethics*, 360.

Concluding Freedom and Will

God's image on the heart of Man is the central point to understanding Man at all. It is that all-important characteristic which guides him through life, gives him his unique, unrepeatable personality, and makes him worthy of dignity. God beckons all of us through the created world and allows us to search for Him in ways specific to us through the subjective experience of the senses. We must be allowed the freedom to pursue God where He calls to us, since He is that Chief Good who makes us happy.

Though *anamnesis* always dictates to us what makes us happy, we *do* have the ability to choose what is against the clear dictates of conscience for a lesser good. When we do so, we thereby inhibit our own ability to choose that which most makes us happy and free. A freedom that is indifferent to good and evil choices is isolating, entrapping Man in a nightmarish chaos he tries to create for himself. We must remain fixed on cooperation with the Holy Spirit in the working of our own hearts, for He continues to call to us even when we reject Him.

In the final analysis, we consign ourselves to a world of torment and self-loathing by rejecting that which truly makes us happy. This state of torment is brought on by the constant confrontation of our rejecting that which is so deeply a part of our being. We cannot fail *but* be made happy by it—even when we do not recognize it anymore. The torment that the final kiss God gives to us in the throes of our own nightmarish creation is captured so strikingly by the final movement of the Grand Inquisitor at the end of the story:

> When the Inquisitor stopped speaking, he waited some time for his prisoner to answer him. His silence weighed down upon him. He saw that the prisoner had listened intently and calmly all the time, looking gently in his face and evidently not wishing to reply. The old man longed for Him to say something, however bitter and terrible. But He suddenly approaches the old man in silence and softly kisses him on his bloodless aged lips. That was His whole answer. The old man shudders. Something trembles at the edge of his

lips . . . The kiss burns in his heart, but
the old man adheres to his idea.[198]

---

198. Dostoyevsky, "The Grand Inquisitor."
This is such a moving image. Blavatsky's translation is very similar; even so, there are some minor language variations of different emphases which prompt us to offer her translation as well:
"Having disburdened his heart, the Inquisitor waits for some time to hear his prisoner speak in His turn. His silence weighs upon him. He has seen that his captive has been attentively listening to him all the time, with His eyes fixed penetratingly and softly on the face of his jailer, and evidently bent upon not replying to him. The old man longs to hear His voice, to hear Him reply; better words of bitterness and scorn than His silence. Suddenly He rises; slowly and silently approaching the Inquisitor, He bends towards him and softly kisses the bloodless, four-score-and-ten-year-old lips. That is all the answer. The Grand Inquisitor shudders. There is a convulsive twitch at the corner of his mouth . . . The kiss burns his heart, but the old man remains firm in his own ideas and unbelief."

Concluding this Book: On Being Right

"Sometimes what you think is an end is only a beginning. And that wouldn't do at all." Agatha Christie, *(Death comes as the End, 1944)*

I have found that closing a book is the hardest part of the whole process. As the time comes to begin putting words to paper, I am veritably plagued with fears, worries, and doubts. Have I accurately and sufficiently made my case? Is it worth making this particular case in the first place? Have I missed anything crucial? Have I accurately represented the thoughts of those I have relied upon? And, possibly most damning of all, "*Am I right?*"

This last question is the final point of discussion I would like to focus on. I close this book with this examination, not so much that my own fears might be alleviated, but more so that anyone who reads this book might not enter into the newly rediscovered world of debate with a fatally erroneous stance toward their own articulations. This book is, after all, an anthropological, epistemological, and philosophical starting point from which conversations surrounding freedom, personhood, individuality, and the framework of reality itself can evolve.

The premise of any argument is of such profound weight that if it is faulty, the logical conclusions that follow are often just as *wrong* as they are rationally sound. To return to G. K. Chesterton's *Orthodoxy*, we might observe that "the madman's explanation of a thing is always complete, and often in a purely rational sense satisfactory. Or, to speak more strictly, the insane explanation, if not conclusive, is at least unanswerable."[199] So if my readers are not convinced of the truth of my argument, you may be tempted to suppose that all you have done is waste your time in reading something which will *not* equip you for further discussions. I must show at least *some* mark of having spoken the truth, and not merely spewing rationales from my own insurmountable subjective experience.

Perhaps even more fundamental than defending my own stance, however, this conclusion ought to provide a sort of recap of the whole overarching argument. A cathartic close to the conversation preceding, as it were.

---

199. Chesterton, *Orthodoxy*, 11.

And, luckily for me, tackling the radical subjectivity of the human experience and relating it to both the objective truth *and* other persons around us has been at the forefront of our conversation. In fact, as far as logical progression goes, a formal treating of Man's communal nature and a practical application of the personalistic norm and what Man's state as a *gendered creature* seems to be the next step. Alas! There is only so much room in this current project to tackle such things. Stay tuned for a continuation of the conversation!

The thesis of this book can really be summed up in one sentence: Man is, at his core, an essentially *communal*—not isolated—animal and can only encounter reality or come to knowledge as relational to and encountering another subject—THE Subject, God, specifically. The modern world would have every individual left to their own interpretations of data, which occurs only to them, and has no metric by which we can be sure we are right. Open-mindedness, for those trapped in the absurdities of the Enlightenment, is then nothing but doubt of perceived truth as potentially—but unverifiably—simply the product of my own psyche. "At any street corner," Chesterton astutely observes, "we may meet a man who utters the frantic and blasphemous statement that he may be wrong. Everyday one comes across somebody who says that of course his view may not be the right one. Of course his view must be the right one, or it is not his view."[200] Without

200. Chesterton, *Orthodoxy*, 24.

reference to God as Creator and preserver even of our subjective senses, this modern view is the only coherent conclusion—despite its absurdity.

The evidence for the truth of this first statement, that Man is communal and comes to *know* only in relation to another subject, is manifest through our discussion. Man desires to know, he can only know through his senses, and his senses are aimed at one thing: allowing him to choose the good and live according to truth so that his life might be beautiful. This is God, who creates and preserves our subjectivity through our senses and speaks to us particularly through them. If we were not relational beings, if we did not find fulfillment in an encounter with another subject outside of our own autonomy, we would not *seek* others. We would attempt to choose our own good and would rightly regard God's intervention as an unjust imposition on our individuality. This conclusion, within the framework of teleology, is simply untenable.

Teleology plays an important role in our conversation, and indeed in detecting coherency in the cosmos. In this light, there is a second follow-up sentence which I suppose sums up the ramification of the articulated thesis: We can know something is *rational* (and therefore aimed at truth) not inasmuch as it is logically consistent in its internal argument but rather when it is aimed at beholding the order of the cosmos—and when it is the function of a *subject* understanding the cosmos. Reason, in isolation, is maddening and further isolates the individual. Again, leaning on Chesterton, "We may say in summary that [the chief mark and element of insanity is] reason used without root, reason in a void. The man who begins to think without the proper first principles goes mad; he begins to think at the wrong end."[201]

There is no subjectivity in the madman Chesterton describes. He is not someone who perceives the world and acts upon it with his own aims, seeking to understand the cosmos and to live according to the true and the good. The madman is an autonomous robotlike calculator, whose every action is dictated by some other data along the string of occurrences that has led to this moment. Rather than determine the truth through *dialectic* and live as a response to that truth, the madman is a victim to the data of his own logic. Reason must be aimed at understanding, and understanding is aimed at beholding God as Person. In other words, *Ratio must have intellectus as its aim.*

Does this book bear the marks of being correct? I would posit yes. However, the truth of the preceding pages will be up to the reader to discuss, weigh, and determine. While I have intended and attempted to represent the truth to the best of my ability, carefully weaving thinkers like Pieper, Pope John Paul II, Ratzinger, Pinckaers, and McIntyre together to form a tapestry reflecting reality, truth often becomes manifest through discussion. That is the whole point of relying

201. Chesterton, *Orthodoxy*, 20.

on other authors' works in the first place: entering into discussion with those giants who have already come before.

In a discussion, two or more subjects aim at the same truth through discourse with each other, thereby elevating their reason beyond the calculations of madmen and machines and into the realm of the human, aimed at the divine. Discussion is the epitome of rational activity, for it is in discussion that reason has a proximate experience with its oriented goal: beholding of another subject and His revelation of Himself. To this end, I hope the reader sees fit to discuss these pages with others so that their merit might become apparent. In any event, I have tried to cultivate even within these pages an atmosphere of discursive tone.

Discussion is precisely what is lacking in the world today, and why so many absurdist claims are gaining traction among thinkers and doers alike. When each individual becomes isolated in their own data collection/interpretation, there is no encounter with another and reason becomes mere categorization of perception. These categorizations are as invincible to outside refutation as they are isolating for the individual. The response to this phenomenon, Chesterton suggests, isn't so much to *refute* the individual as much as it is to merely *extract* him from his own insanity—to allow him to encounter another subject. He writes:

> If we attempt to trace [error of insanity/pure reason] in exact terms, we

> shall not find it quite so easy as we had supposed. Perhaps the nearest we can get to expressing it is to say this: that [the mind so plaqued] moves in a perfect but narrow circle. A small circle is quite as infinite as a large circle; but, though it is quite as infinite, it is not so large. In the same way the insane explanation is quite as complete as the sane one, but it is not so large . . . The lunatic's theory explains a large number of things, but it does not explain them in a large way. I mean that if you or I were dealing with a mind that was growing morbid, we should be chiefly concerned not so much to give it arguments as to give it air, to convince it that there was something cleaner and cooler outside the suffocation of a single argument.[202]

Encounter, not conquering, is the aim of reason. If we, as a society, can reclaim this, many of the absurdities in our intellectual spheres will dissipate. Not only that: Many of the societal ills will fade away into distant memory, too. Suicide, euthanasia, rampant addictions to alcohol, drugs, and pornography, all these become solvable problems when we forsake the notion of individual categorization, the theory that I can determine what I am allowed to do and am licensed to do what I can get away with, if only I do no harm to another person. When we stop becoming individuals in our own subjective worlds, we can encounter and live

202. Chesterton, *Orthodoxy*, 12.

together out in the *real* world, the world which encompasses the whole of reality.

Let us be Men; let us cease to be crows.

Bibliography

Aquinas, Thomas. *Summa Theologiae*.

Aristotle. *De Anima.* In *The Basic Works of Aristotle,* edited by Richard McKeon. New York: Modern Library, 2001.

———. *Metaphysics.* In *The Basic Works of Aristotle,* edited by Richard McKeon. New York: Modern Library, 2001.

———. *The Nicomachean Ethics.* In *The Basic Works of Aristotle,* edited by Richard McKeon. New York: Modern Library, 2001.

———. *Politics.* In *The Basic Works of Aristotle,* edited by Richard McKeon. New York: Modern Library, 2001.

Augustine. *Confessions.* Translated by Henry Chadwick. Oxford: Oxford University Press, 2008.

———. *De Trinitate*.

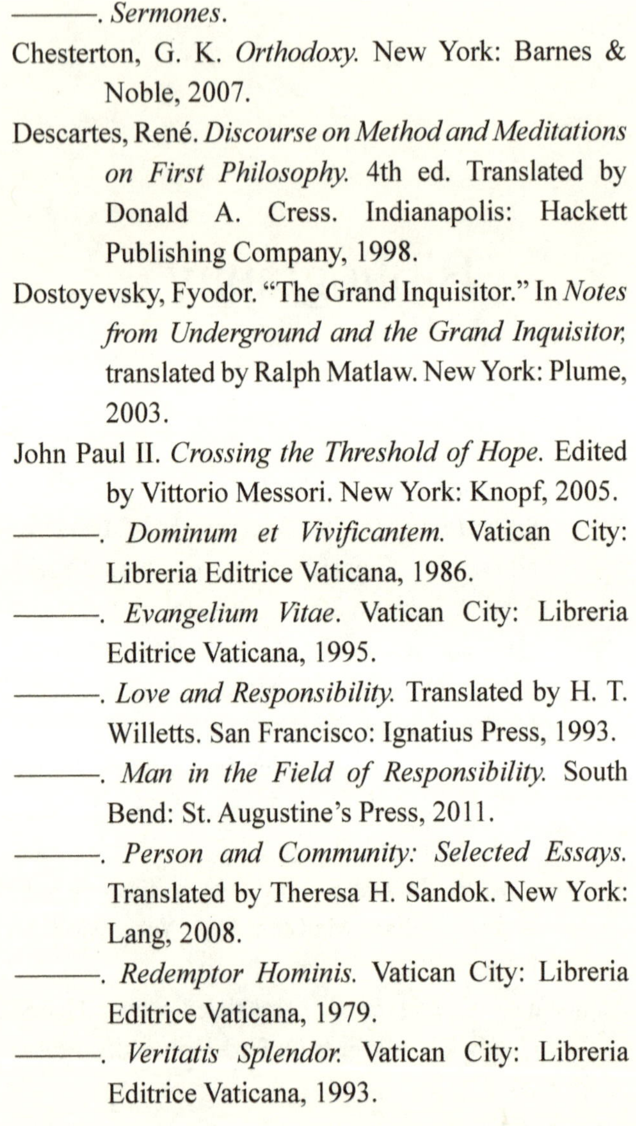

———. *Sermones.*

Chesterton, G. K. *Orthodoxy.* New York: Barnes & Noble, 2007.

Descartes, René. *Discourse on Method and Meditations on First Philosophy.* 4th ed. Translated by Donald A. Cress. Indianapolis: Hackett Publishing Company, 1998.

Dostoyevsky, Fyodor. "The Grand Inquisitor." In *Notes from Underground and the Grand Inquisitor,* translated by Ralph Matlaw. New York: Plume, 2003.

John Paul II. *Crossing the Threshold of Hope.* Edited by Vittorio Messori. New York: Knopf, 2005.

———. *Dominum et Vivificantem.* Vatican City: Libreria Editrice Vaticana, 1986.

———. *Evangelium Vitae.* Vatican City: Libreria Editrice Vaticana, 1995.

———. *Love and Responsibility.* Translated by H. T. Willetts. San Francisco: Ignatius Press, 1993.

———. *Man in the Field of Responsibility.* South Bend: St. Augustine's Press, 2011.

———. *Person and Community: Selected Essays.* Translated by Theresa H. Sandok. New York: Lang, 2008.

———. *Redemptor Hominis.* Vatican City: Libreria Editrice Vaticana, 1979.

———. *Veritatis Splendor.* Vatican City: Libreria Editrice Vaticana, 1993.

Kant, Immanuel. *Prolegomena to Any Future Metaphysics: And the Letter to Marcus Herz, February 1772.* Translated by James W. Ellington. Indianapolis: Hackett Publishing Company, 2010.

MacIntyre, Alasdair. *After Virtue: A Study in Moral Theory.* 3rd ed. Notre Dame: University of Notre Dame Press, 2007.

Martyr, Justin. *First Apology.* In *The First and Second Apologies,* translated by Leslie W. Barnard. New York: Paulist Press, 1997.

Pico Della Mirandola, Giovanni. *On the Dignity of Man.* Indianapolis: Hackett Publishing Company, 1998.

Pieper, Josef. *Leisure: The Basis of Culture,* Including *The Philosophical Act.* San Francisco: Ignatius Press, 2009.

Pinckaers, Servais. *The Sources of Christian Ethics.* Translated by Mary Thomas Noble. Edinburgh: T&T Clark, 2001.

Plato. *Meno.* In *The Essential Plato,* translated by Benjamin Jowett and M. J. Knight. New York: Quality Paperback Book Club, 1999.

———. *Phaedo.* In *The Essential Plato,* translated by Benjamin Jowett and M. J. Knight. New York: Quality Paperback Book Club, 1999.

———. *Phaedrus.* In *The Essential Plato,* translated by Benjamin Jowett and M. J. Knight. New York: Quality Paperback Book Club, 1999.

———. *The Republic.* In *The Essential Plato,* translated by Benjamin Jowett and M. J. Knight. New York: Quality Paperback Book Club, 1999.

Qadri, Haseeb Mehmood, Saima Mushtaq, Syed Muhammad S. Qadri, et al. "Physiological, Psychosocial and Substance Abuse Effects of Pornography Addiction: A Narrative Review." *Cureus* 15, no. 1 (January 2023): e33682. https://doi.org/10.7759/cureus.33682.

Ratzinger, Joseph. *On Conscience: Two Essays.* San Francisco: Ignatius Press, 2007.

Ripperger, Chad. *Dominion: The Nature of Diabolical Warfare.* Keenesburg: Sensus Traditionis Press, 2022.

Sophocles. *Oedipus Rex.* Translated by Sir George Young. Mineola: Dover Publications, 2012.

Wojtyła, Karol. *Person and Community: Selected Essays.* Catholic Thought from Lublin. Translated by Theresa H. Sandok. New York: Lang, 2008.

About the Author

Connor S. Curley is a hog farmer-turned philosopher, originally hailing from Bethune, SC. He earne his undergraduate in Liberal Arts from Magdalen College in Warner, NH and his MA in JPII studies from the John Paul II Institute out of the University of St. Thomas, Houston. Many of his writings are featured on Catholic365, as well as his personal Substack, *Remembering Tomorrow*. He has taught Drama, Latin, and Theology in different capacities over the years. He has been a guest on Relevant Radio's *The Drew Mariani Show*, and has been known to maintain a hefty presence in the comment sections of various online publications.

Mr. Curley has spent much of his professional career in the military/security fields. He spent several years driving armored cars, and as an 8-year member of the National Guard has deployed twice in support of the Southwest Border Mission. He spent two years assigned as a member of the Homeland Response Force, and most recently has spent several years as a recruiter for the National Guard.

Mr. Curley currently resides in Ohio with his wife and their son. He enjoys playing the banjo, spending time outside as a family, and engaging in impactful discussions over an evening glass of bourbon - preferably Horse Soldier, and preferably around a fire. The Curley home is often the backdrop for formally hosted discussions on Tradition, Faith matters, Gender Norms, and Anthropology, to name a few.

Index

I

J

K

L

M

O

P

R

S

T

www.ingramcontent.com/pod-product-compliance
Lightning Source LLC
LaVergne TN
LVHW091040080826
845145LV00002B/567

* 9 7 8 1 6 3 3 5 7 4 8 3 0 *